FINDING FAITH
in the Storm

ENDORSEMENTS

Pebbles's memoir is a testament to the human spirit encountering God in the most difficult trials. Throughout her lifelong chronic condition, she discovers that "we don't get through by working harder but by learning to rest better." When Pebbles rests in the Lord, she realizes that although the physical, emotional, and spiritual pain will continue in her present life, she is able to carry her cross because her Savior is carrying it with her. Her life is a tangible reminder that God is in the details and none of us need to be strong and work harder. By our very brokenness, we allow Jesus to be "strong in me."
—Dr. Penny McCann-Washer, PhD in Rhetoric and Composition, Indiana Wesleyan University

This remarkable story tells of a life that should have ended more than once and was filled with pain and disappointment. But Pebbles's story is not one of despair, but one of redemption, determination, hope, love, and accomplishment. When Pebbles was my student, I witnessed her determination and resolve to succeed against all odds. She was one of the most determined and successful students I have known—often completing her assignments with excellence and on time from her hospital

bed. Pebbles is an overcomer! With tenacious resolve, love from friends and blessings from her Lord and Savior, her life is a living triumph! Read and be inspired as I was!
—**Dr. Henry Smith**, PhD, President Emeritus Indiana Wesleyan University

As I read *Finding Faith in the Storm*, I was overwhelmed by the strength of spirit, the determination and the blessings Pebbles's life has given to those who have met her. She is an example of God's love walking and talking. So many moments that might have shattered someone else, but she has continued to blossom and bring joy to a world that needs it so much. Well worth the read and may she continue to shine for many years to come.
—**Gina Brisco**, President, Gaither Management Group, Inc.

FINDING FAITH
in the Storm

PEBBLES WIREMAN

A Christian Company
ElkLakePublishingInc.com

COPYRIGHT NOTICE

Finding Faith in the Storm

First edition. Copyright © 2024 by Pebbles Wireman. The information contained in this book is the intellectual property of Pebbles Wireman and is governed by United States and International copyright laws. All rights reserved. No part of this publication, either text or image, may be used for any purpose other than personal use. Therefore, reproduction, modification, storage in a retrieval system, or retransmission, in any form or by any means, electronic, mechanical, or otherwise, for reasons other than personal use, except for brief quotations for reviews or articles and promotions, is strictly prohibited without prior written permission by the publisher.

NO AI TRAINING: Without in any way limiting the Pebbles Wireman and publisher's exclusive rights under copyright, any use of this publication to "train" generative artificial intelligence (AI) technologies to generate text is expressly prohibited. The author reserves all rights to license uses of this work for generative AI training and development of machine learning language models.

Unless otherwise indicated, all Scripture quotations are from the ESV® Bible (The Holy Bible, English Standard Version®), copyright© 2001 by Crossway Bibles, a publishing ministry of Good News Publishers. Used by permission. All rights reserved.

Scriptures marked NIV are taken from the NEW INTERNATIONAL VERSION (NIV):Scripture taken from THE HOLY BIBLE, NEW INTERNATIONAL VERSION ®. Copyright© 1973, 1978, 1984, 2011 by Biblica, Inc.™. Used by permission of Zondervan.

FINDING FAITH IN THE STORM VII

"All to Jesus I Surrender," Judson W. Van DeVenter, public domain.

Cover and Interior Design: Kelly Artieri, Deb Haggerty
Editor(s): Jeanne Marie Leach, Judy Hagey, Deb Haggerty

PUBLISHED BY: Elk Lake Publishing, Inc., 35 Dogwood Drive, Plymouth, MA 02360, 2024

Library Cataloging Data

Names: Wireman, Pebbles (Pebbles Wireman)

Finding Faith in the Storm / Pebbles, Wireman

152 p. 23cm × 15cm (9in × 6 in.)

ISBN-13: 9798891342460 (paperback) | 9798891342477 (trade paperback) | 9798891342484 (e-book)

Key Words:Christian women's challenges overcoming illness; Jesus recovery memoir brain injury woman faith; Faith-based healing traumatic injury woman God;Season of change Christ comfort for women; Inspirational coping journey Christian women; Renewed identity God women after disability; Spirituality faith disability woman self-help

Library of Congress Control Number: 2024945711 Nonfiction

DEDICATION

I dedicate this book to each of you who found a place on the page. God has used each of you differently but all of you significantly. I also dedicate this book to the ones who were not mentioned. Although your names may not meet the pages of this book, they are embedded in my heart. Every person I have met along the way has touched my life in some way.

I do not want to forget my doctors, nurses, and medical team, who continue to battle with me toward my healing and living the best life I can despite my illnesses.

Over the years, God has placed just the right people in my life at just the right season. Each of them has played a significant role in helping me get to where I am today.

But most of all, I want to thank my heavenly Father for guiding, directing, and using me along the journey to *Finding Faith in the Storm*!

TABLE OF CONTENTS

Dedication	ix
Foreword	xiii
Acknowledgments	xv
Chapter 1	1
Chapter 2	11
Chapter 3	21
Chapter 4	29
Chapter 5	39
Chapter 6	47
Chapter 7	61
Chapter 8	73
Chapter 9	87
Chapter 10	99
Chapter 11	105
Chapter 12	113
Chapter 13	119
Chapter 14	125
About the Author	135

FOREWORD

Sometimes, you know when God brings people into your life for reasons not always understood but ultimately for His glory.

That is certainly true when God arranged for me to be the first one on the scene of that fatal accident in 1991, later to learn of her name only as "Pebbles."

After reconnecting nearly twenty years later in a church service, I knew only God could orchestrate such circumstances.

I have watched Pebbles go through years of seemingly countless surgeries and continued suffering, only to witness strength and perseverance that only God can give.

I am certain that this book will encourage many people to find faith as they go through their own storm.

—**Debra Chizum**, Bachelor of Arts Biblical Counseling

ACKNOWLEDGMENTS

I want to thank everyone who believed in me, encouraged me, and loved me along the path to achieving what I felt was impossible by finishing this book.

When Deb Haggerty at Elk Lake Publishing said she would like me to begin by writing my memoir, many thoughts and emotions flooded my mind. Why would anyone want to read about me? But it was not at all about me—it was about God and what He has done in my life. I faced many storms while completing this book, but Deb continued to believe in me and encouraged me along the way. She helped me see beyond the storms to the Light that guided me along the way. Thank you, Deb, for helping me achieve the impossible.

My book would not be complete without the words contributed by Debra Chizum, who shared the memories that lived on in her heart after the day she saw my life being changed forever. She shared a part of the story I had no memory of, but it affected my life forever.

This book is filled with many pages of words that were brought to life by my editor, Judy Hagey. They helped me to dig deeper into the tests in my life and reveal how God used those tests to create testimonies along the way. They brought my words to life and helped me find the strength to share more than I believed I had the strength to share.

I do not want to forget to mention a friend who helped me through the editing process while taking me back and forth to many of my surgeries and procedures. Thank you, Pam Barry, for your continued love, prayers and support.

Most of all, I want to thank my heavenly Father for giving me the words to guide my heart.

We have all gone through storms in our life. Yet, it is by faith that we get through those storms. My prayers are with each of you who pick up this book and read it, that you may find the peace of love of Jesus Christ to carry you through the storms you may face.

May you find faith in the storms of your life.

God is our refuge and strength, an ever-present help in trouble. Therefore we will not fear, though the earth give way and the mountains fall into the heart of the sea, though its waters roar and foam and the mountains quake with their surging. (Psalm 46:1–3)

CHAPTER 1

IS IT A DREAM?

My life was stolen from me the day a drunk driver ran me off the road. My body was thrown from the car as it tumbled into a deep ditch. I awoke in a moment of fog, looking down at all around me. Was this a dream, or was it really happening to me? I do not remember the moments that followed or the moment a stranger, Debra, laid me in the back seat of her car, wiping the blood from my face as she continued praying over me. Lying there, bruised, cut, broken, and bleeding, the sirens overtook the silence that once plagued the air. Police cars, fire trucks, an ambulance, and emergency personnel crowded the road.

Overwhelmed by all that was happening, Debra answered their questions as the EMTs lifted my body from the back seat of her green Buick Park Avenue. The smoldering sun barreled down on my face as they gently laid me on a hard, narrow gurney.

In a state of shock, Debra explained to the officers, "I was on my way home from running errands nearby. As I rounded the curve, I glimpsed a car flipped upside down in the ditch on the side of the road. The wheels were still spinning as I pulled over and reached inside the bulky car phone bag for the phone to call 911. It took me a minute to realize I was the first person to arrive on the scene of the accident.

"While I was on the phone, a young girl covered in blood made her way up the hill to the edge of the road. At that moment, I knew something was wrong. As she neared the top of the embankment, I got a closer look at her. Her face was bruised and bloodied. I knew there was no way she could have made it up that hill on her own. It was as if angels were carrying her."

Debra continued explaining to the officer, "I could not believe what I was seeing! Where did this girl come from? Was she driving that car? Was she all alone? How do I help her?"

To Debra, the victim appeared to be the age of her daughter. Her motherly instinct took over. "I knew I had to help her," Debra continued. "The Holy Spirit guided me. I took her into my arms and led her to the back seat of my car, where I found a white towel. I used the towel to wipe the blood and tears from her face. I sat beside her on the edge of the seat, praying for God's healing touch and intervention as I waited for the ambulance to arrive.

"While the young girl continued to slip in and out of consciousness, I began asking her questions, but got no reply. Then in a moment of silence, she whispered 'Pebbles' just before drifting out of consciousness again. I didn't know if that was her name or what she was referring to. After what seemed like hours, the EMTs arrived and approached my car where her body lay."

The EMTs stabilized me as Debra continued answering their barrage of questions. Struggling to get an IV in, they loaded my body on the gurney, preparing to carry me to the back of the ambulance. As they pulled my body out of the car, they paused for a moment to draw a white sheet over my face to protect me from the bright sun. Just then, a blue Ford Escort pulled up behind Debra's car.

Alarmed by the flashing lights and the sirens, my mom got out of the car just as the EMTs covered my face. Shocked by what appeared to be my last moments, she rushed to the EMT, a family friend who recognized her.

"Your daughter's been severely injured in a car accident," he said. "We're taking her to Plymouth Parkview Hospital. You can follow us."

Mom rushed back to her friend's car. "Follow that ambulance," she ordered.

As the ambulance rounded the curve, the EMTs continued to work on me. Debra glimpsed the bright light shining through the back doors and continued praying as they carried me away. *Would she ever know who that young girl was that she'd tended to moments earlier? Would she ever see that girl again? Was Pebbles her name? Would either of their lives ever be the same again?* The day's scene was etched in her mind while the name Pebbles echoed in her ears. She continued praying faithfully for the young girl who'd touched her life in such a short but significant time.

Much about that day remains a mystery. But one thing I know for sure—God was there from the moment my car veered off the road, flipped three times, throwing me out the window before it settled at the bottom of a deep ditch. God sent His angels to carry me up the hill, and He sent Debra to care for me until the ambulance arrived. God placed Debra there at that very moment to care for me, when I was physically, mentally, and spiritually lost. She was an angel on assignment.

Debra left the accident scene as the ambulance pulled away. Driving down Highway 17 in northwest Indiana, many questions ran through her mind, "How did that girl survive the accident?" How did she get to the top of the hill with all her injuries?" "How did a white towel get laid on the back seat of my car?" Debra may never know the answers to these questions, but she did know God was there guiding and directing her to care for His young daughter. He provided a way when there was no way.

Larry, Debra's husband, was waiting for her at home. She arrived later than expected, carrying a towel stained with blood from a girl she never expected to see again. Tears welled up in her eyes as she explained coming upon the accident as she rounded the curve on Highway 17. Debra shared how she pulled to the edge of the road when she saw a car flipped in the bottom of a ditch with the wheels still spinning. As she edged the car to the side of the road, she caught a glimpse of a young girl alongside the road with blood running down her face. "Her head must have hit or gone through the windshield. She looked like a character from a horror film."

Yet, this was not a horror story. It was not a story at all. This was a moment in her life she would never forget with a girl she would always know as "Pebbles." While the memories flooded her thoughts, prayers continued in her heart. Debra knew that the One who began a good work would be faithful to complete it (Philippians 1:6).

I wish I could say I remember all Debra did for me that day. But I do not recall the moments after my car was forced off the road or even the moments before I was rushed to the hospital, where I was hooked up to many machines. I do, however, remember the pain that plagued my body as I awoke in a hospital bed alone and scared. The loud beeps of the machines echoed in the cold, dark hospital room.

Waking in a moment of confusion, I did not know what had happened to me, where I was, or if I would ever see my family and friends again. I was as afraid of the unknown as much as the known. My life, as I'd known it, was taken from me on that day—even before it had truly begun. Lying there in pain, I wondered if I would ever know what happened to me that day—the day that changed my life forever! The day my hopes and dreams were crushed. Would I ever meet the angel who laid me in the back seat of her car and prayed over me? Was this moment in my life the end or a new beginning?

I slipped in and out of consciousness. Bright lights flooded the room. Doctors and nurses continued to poke and prod me. After finally getting an IV started, they took me from one room to the next, running various tests. The pain overpowered me as they took my body from one table to the another. At one point, they slid me into a long narrow tube where I had to lay perfectly still. Once my entire body was inside, it sounded like people were pounding on the walls with sledgehammers. My head was about to explode. I just wanted them to stop. I wanted everything to stop. I wanted to wake up from this nightmare.

Why can't I wake up?
Why won't this pain stop?
Why won't these people leave me alone?"

Back in my room, shortly after the MRI, I began to slip away. The room became dark.

Where had everyone gone?
What am I doing here?
Who is lying in that bed?

I looked closer and saw a young girl lying there helpless and alone. Me. Doctors and nurses gathered round my bed, talking in loud voices. No one could see me looking down at my body lying limp on the bed. They began pounding on my chest between the shocks that pierced my veins. I was slowly slipping away. I did not want to go, nor did I want to stay. I just wanted to cry as fear engulfed me.

Lying in the cold, dark room, I feared all around me. The noise took over my thoughts, and the pain consumed my body. "What was going to happen to me?" "Why do these people keep poking me and hurting me?" "Why don't they smile?" "I do not want to be here; I do not want them to keep hurting me." "Why can't I wake up from this dream?"

I did not think I would ever wake up again. I did not know if my body would recover from all it had endured. "Where would my life go from here?" "How would I ever live with the pain?" Everything seemed impossible at that moment. With a push of the IV, I got a moment's relief and a bit of hope, only to have the pain return moments later with a vengeance.

Minutes seemed like hours, and hours like days. I hoped the short, brown-haired lady from the accident would walk through the door. The lady with the gentle spirit and sweet smile who whispered hope, peace, and healing over me. Although she didn't come through the hospital doors, she did continue to pray for me. Her prayers remained forever embedded in my heart.

Days later, I was released from the hospital with a traumatic brain injury, broken bones, whiplash, cuts, bruises, and orders for lots of physical therapy. Medical personnel finished the paperwork as my mom walked through the hospital room doors, ready to take me home. Pain overwhelmed my body while fear and anxiety overpowered my mind. A nurse wheeled me to my mom's car and loaded me into the back seat. The sun was scorching hot, and the car had no air conditioning. With the window rolled down and the sun beating in, the sweat poured down my face, drenching my neck brace, sling, knee brace, and other bandages.

The five-mile trip home seemed like thousands of miles. My pain intensified and consumed me with each bump in the road and every turn. I was relieved to finally reach home but I was angry. Angry that I could not do anything! Angry that the pain was too much to bear! Angry that my senior year would no longer be the same! Angry that I would spend my summer in physical therapy instead of on a beach with my friends! Angry that my life had been stolen from me the day a drunk driver ran me off the road.

I tried to paint a picture of what I felt that day, but there were no colors to portray the emotions hidden deep inside me. There was no color hot enough to show my burning pain. No color bright enough to make me feel joy again. No color dark enough to show my deepest despair. There was just a thin, tattered, torn line on the page representing a single thread of hope.

The night passed slowly as pain consumed my body, and flashbacks consumed my mind. Light peeked through the window. I heard the birds chirping and saw the squirrels gathering walnuts. All ordinary things. But nothing would ever be ordinary for me again.

Tired, hurt, and depressed, I had to prepare for physical therapy. I did not want to return to the hospital, not for a day or moment, especially not for physical therapy. I knew the pain I was about to face and knew there was no way out. With crutches in hand, my arm in a sling, and my neck in a brace, I was ready to face the day I dreaded and did not know how to endure.

My mom dropped me off in front of the hospital. I hobbled from the car to the electronic doors, where I met Rosie, my physical therapist. Her whimsical socks and warm smile did not prepare me for the grueling workout she put me through. Despite her fun-loving personality, Rosie pushed me harder and harder with each session—almost to the breaking point. Undeterred by my tears, Rosie would not let me quit. She made me face the pain head on, pushing me to the limit of more than I thought I could bear. The pain overwhelmed my body and my mind. She hardly gave me a moment to breathe before she said, "Do it again. Again. Just once more."

I did not have the strength or the willpower to do it on my own, but Rosie never lost faith in me. She knew I could do it and had to do it to reach the point that would break away all that held me back from recovering and living a life of hope and possibilities. When I was released from PT after several months, saying goodbye was as hard as saying hello because now I knew Rosie cared about me and my recovery.

Those countless hours of physical therapy prepared me for the first day of my senior year—the day I had worked toward all my life. Although Rosie and PT prepared me physically, nothing had prepared me mentally for this day. Nothing was as I'd envisioned it. Returning to class with the scars of my accident still evident was not what I had hoped for or planned. The accident changed everything, including my friends.

Emotions flooded my mind as I walked through the crowd of students to reach the big glass doors at the entrance to the school. Although I had been here many times before, this day seemed like the first time. Nothing protected me from the silent stares and the whispers of my classmates. The friends I had known most of my life had become distant strangers. Walking with a limp, I tried to hide behind my broken nose and bruises. With my arm in a sling, I struggled to carry my books. No one offered to help me. Even though I was the girl they had known for most of their lives, they gawked at me as if I had a contagious disease.

While I did not look the same on the outside, I had not changed on the inside. I was the same girl who sang in the choir, competed on the speech team, and participated in other school activities just months before. But my classmates acted like they didn't know me. Yet, I could not blame them because they did not know what to say or how to act.

As I made my way to my first class, I began to feel the pain and isolation so many students have felt over the years. I realized the cliff that divided the invisible from the visible. Why hadn't I ever seen that deep, dark cliff before? Why hadn't I tried to build a bridge? Why did there have to be a divide? Things were not supposed to be like this.

As if the scars from the accident were not enough, the announcement that came over the loudspeaker that day was worse. "Don't forget to sign up for your senior pictures." My face still bore bruises from the accident. My broken nose was still healing. Tears welled up as I understood how the accident had affected every part of my life. To some, a senior picture may be just a picture. But to me, it was a legacy of all I'd achieved in the last eleven years. Now that legacy would be overshadowed by the many broken pieces of my life.

Not only did I skip getting my senior pictures taken, I also skipped our class photo, something I still regret. The scars on my face did not define who I was but represented a piece of my life that helped me become who I am today.

Months later, after the wounds on my face had healed, my mom had a family friend take my senior pictures. They were beautiful; they were everything I could have ever wanted. The photos portrayed the girl the students had always known. Yet, they did not reflect who I had become. No longer the girl they once knew, I was battling to find my identity. Lost in a crowd where I once belonged, wanting to hide from my past and run from my present. But where would I go to escape the prison I felt I was in? I did not know who I was anymore or even who I had been. Lost to myself and battling obstacles in my relationship with my parents, I left home in the middle of my senior year. No one understood me! But how could they when I did not understand myself?

At the same time as I was recovering from my accident, my parents were dealing with my older sister. In addition to her split personality, she battled many addictions. Getting help for her became their focus, even to the point of losing their other children. My brother gave up his activities and time with his friends to care for her son and keep him safe. Everyone in my family gave up a meaningful piece of their life to save one who didn't want to be saved.

Something changed in me through all this. I struggled to make it through my senior year. Going through something so traumatic changes who you are and how you see the world around you. Many say things they don't really mean or understand. Some said they understood all I was going through. I know now they meant well, but unless you've walked in another's shoes you cannot really know what they are going through. How could they understand me and all I had gone through when I didn't understand myself? I was at a place where I did not know how to trust a God I did not know.

CHAPTER 2

IT'S OK NOT TO BE OK

I have learned that it's OK not to be OK. No matter how hard I try, I can't escape the pain that consumes me or get back the life that was taken from me. During my recovery, some friendships and bonds grew stronger while others grew further apart. I found myself asking what I'd done to deserve this but had no clear answer or solution. My heart became bitter as remembered all I'd lost: my family, friends, school, and everything I'd ever known.

Trying to overcome the bitterness, I began to focus on the positive.

I was positively sure I would never get my life back.

I was positive everything had been taken from me.

I was positive that I didn't want to be positive.

I still had a lot of work to do to become more positive.

As a child, I was independent and always knew what I wanted, or at least I thought I did. Yet my life was no longer my own. During the day, I tried to figure out where I belonged. Nights were filled with loneliness and despair. I was constantly searching for what was missing and trying to find my place in this world.

While my parents focused on saving my sister, they grew distant from me. I longed for their love and attention.

I longed to have a life of my own instead of one consumed by my sister and her destructive lifestyle. I was searching for love and acceptance in a home that was filled with brokenness. My mom was married several times before marrying the love of her life. As a result, I was one of a family of sixteen kids. Although she was happy, and her husband treated her like a queen, I missed my dad and my brothers who'd moved with him. I felt abandoned by those I loved and left with a sister who consumed my mom's every waking moment.

No one in my family understood me or all I was going through. Two months after going back to school, in October of my senior year, I was still struggling to find my way. I felt alone and abandoned by all I knew. I began searching for a place where I would feel accepted and loved. So one night, I left home with a bag of clothes over my back and a backpack filled with schoolwork. I didn't know where I was going or how I'd get there. Tears caressed my face and turned to mud, as I walked down our long, dusty, dirt road. All my hopes and dreams had been crushed the day of my accident. Now I was stranded in the middle of nowhere, asking, "Where do I belong?" Lost in the world of the unknown, my life became a stranger to me.

Afraid of the darkness that overpowered the night, I knocked on a neighbor's door as the cold, crisp October air sent chills down my spine. With my body shaking and teeth quivering, I could barely mumble any words. In almost a whisper, I asked to use the phone. I didn't know who to call. Who could save me from this horrible nightmare? My legs burned; my head was spinning, while my heart was breaking.

With a gentle smile and hug, the lady invited me in to use the phone. She was a family friend who I often babysat for. She knew the pain I had endured and why I felt so alone, yet she did not know how to help. She offered a warm cup of tea as we sat at the table and talked. Knowing I was determined to leave, she offered to let me use her phone.

I picked up the phone and dialed Grace's number, an elderly woman from work whom I'd gone to church with a few days ago. Her number was the only one I knew by heart. With a tenderness in her voice, Grace answered the phone. Without hesitation, she said she would be right there. She knew about the accident and the struggles with my sister.

Gazing out the window, I spotted two bright headlights pulling into the driveway. I slid into the passenger seat of Grace's blue Grand Am. Uncertainty and loneliness joined me. *Where was I going? Where do I belong?* Grace drove slowly down the curving, country road. My heart ripped into pieces as we drove past my parents' home. I wanted to go back. Although my room was there and all my belongings, I could no longer face the continual stress from my sister's destructive behavior while trying to recover from the mental and emotional injuries of my accident.

We turned off Tulip Road and headed toward town. Seconds turned into minutes, and minutes turned into hours as we drove to her two-story white house in the middle of town. Unloading what little I had of my life over my shoulder, I walked toward the four, cracked concrete steps that led to her screened-in porch.

I was moving into another unknown world—another place I didn't really belong. From the screened-in porch, we entered a small living room with an old, brick fireplace. The aroma of cedar-scented wood filled the cozy room.

Gazing into the flames, I lost myself in the moment as Grace prepared hot chocolate to warm me up. I cuddled in front of the fire with a blanket wrapped around my shoulders, watching the flames dance. I tried to escape the emotions built up inside. My fears turned to tears, and my heart was broken in two. I no longer knew what to do. Where would I go, and how would I ever make it alone?

Gentle worship music caressed the air as Grace shared her faith with me. Her life had been much like mine. She was constantly searching for a place to belong until the day she asked Jesus to come into her heart. She knew then that He was who she'd always been searching for.

We talked into the wee hours of the morning until tears gave way to yawns. Together we gathered the bags that held all my life, and Grace led me through the kitchen to a door hidden behind the table and up narrow, creaky stairs to a cold, dark attic. At the top of the steps was a room with an antique bed tucked along the far wall. The space reminded me of an orphanage. At that moment, I felt like an orphan no one wanted.

I unpacked my small duffle bag and changed into my pink, ruffly pajamas. Then I retrieved my brown teddy bear and clutched it to my chest as I crawled under the layers of covers, pulling them up almost over my face.

Lying there awake, paralyzed by fear, I heard the creaking of the house settling and saw shadows creep across the walls as cars passed by. The hours passed by slowly until the sun peeked through the lone, small, round window above the bed where I lay.

In the morning, I woke to the creak of footsteps drawing near. I feared what the day would hold, where I'd go. My body was cold and trembling, and my throat was sore and raspy. As Grace approached my bed, she noticed I was not feeling well. She took my temperature—104.3—and rushed me to the emergency room. My temperature continued to rise as they ran multiple tests.

I was filled with fear as medical personnel continued to poke me. I wanted to call my mom but was afraid to. I lay there in pain and couldn't get warm. My body trembled as the temperature rose. Again, the staff struggled to get an IV into my arm as the machines continued to beep, and staff ran countless tests.

Finally, a doctor appeared in the doorway. He stood at a distance with a mask, gloves, and a paper gown. From there he announced my diagnosis: a rare, contagious disease called Epstein-Barr virus. I saw his mouth move, but I could no longer hear or understand the words he was saying. They clouded my mind.

Why was all this happening to me? Why was I being punished?

My condition worsened throughout the day. I went into a delirium and didn't remember much of that day or the days to follow. They continued to give me IV fluids and antibiotics with only a mild improvement.

I was alone and isolated in a cold hospital room where no one was allowed to visit and nurses and staff avoided me. Not only is Epstein-Barr virus contagious, but it also attacks the immune system, leaving me with an autoimmune disorder. As this occurred only months after my car accident, my body was too weak to fight the disease. With strength only to sleep, I dozed on and off throughout the day. Once again, I felt as if I'd been abandoned by the world.

Weeks went by, and I eventually regained enough strength to go home. But where was home? Where would I go?

As I was still too sick to find a place to stay, my friend Grace took me back to her home, where I remained isolated and hidden in the dark attic with its ox-eye window overlooking the bed. The window was too high to see out, and I was too sick to care. I lay there alone and scared as if I were in prison. Several more days passed before my fever finally broke. No longer contagious, I gained enough strength to look at the piles of homework left at the top of the stairs for me. The mountains of calculus, economics, accounting, and other subjects boggled my brain.

My head was foggy, and my strength weak as I stared at the textbooks in front of me. I couldn't lift them, let alone read them. How would I ever finish my homework? How would I ever graduate? How would I ever get back the life that had been stolen from me?

Nevertheless, I worked hard to excel in my studies in preparation for graduation day. I did all I could to get ready for that day to walk to the sound of "Pomp and Circumstance." The song echoed in my ears as I stepped closer and closer to the finish line. I worked constantly on my studies, trying to catch up on months of work in only a few weeks.

Working on one class at a time wasn't enough as my body was consumed with pain, and my mind was overpowered by mental fog. Suddenly, the song grew dim as I grew further away from the line that was once right in front of me. The goal I had worked all my life to achieve had now become a distant dream.

While most of the teachers had compassion and worked with me, one teacher refused to let the high school counselor give me the makeup tests or even bring the assignments to me at the hospital when I was admitted for about a week. I got further behind as I tried to heal and regain my strength.

I returned to school weeks later. Shortly after that, I lost a dear classmate, Kiara, in a fatal car accident. Our class was devastated by the tragic loss. Kiara was a friend to everyone; she knew no stranger. Her faith touched many lives over the years. Always wearing a radiant smile, she sang like an angel. Our class struggled to grieve the loss of someone so dear. Preparing for graduation no longer seemed important as we attended the funeral of a lifelong friend and classmate.

As I arrived at the church, the line wrapped around the building. The family had reserved a space for Kiara's class, so we walked into the sanctuary as Kiara's voice radiated through the church speakers playing a song she'd recorded a few months before. Tears flowed down my cheeks, and the words comforted my heart as the song was a testimony to all she knew. Her life emulated the love of Jesus. In Kiara's death, many lives were touched and changed that day.

Although her heart stopped beating, she lives on in the hearts of those who knew and loved her. The altar was filled as students dedicated their lives to Jesus. She was a beacon of light to all she knew and many others. She lived the life God had called her to live. "Let your light shine before others, so that they may see your good works and give glory to your Father who is in heaven" (Matthew 5:16).

I was inspired to carry that Light with me that day as I left the altar. This Light will always live inside of me, illuminating most brightly in the darkness, as it did when we returned to the cold, dark hallways of Plymouth High School.

Pain and grief filled the air as the visions and memories of Kiara Joy painted the halls. Her smile had radiated down the hallways, and her angelic voice faded to silence. The silence trembled in the air as we prepared for graduation. The loss weighed us down. We lost more than a classmate that day. We missed Kiara's joy that linked so many of us and the glue of her spirit that bound us together as a class.

Our choir director of many years, Mr. Pickell, reminded us that Kiara was there with us in spirit. He collaborated with us to prepare a song to pay tribute to her and her life. Tears cascaded down our faces as we sang "Friends" by Michael W Smith. The lyrics reminded me that friends are forever if the Lord is in their hearts. Kiara will remain a friend in our hearts as she sings with the angels now.

A few days before graduation, we walked to the gym to rehearse the songs we'd sing as a class to solidify all our accomplishments. The guidance counselor pulled me aside as we approached the gymnasium door. She took me to her office on the other side of the building. I could feel a heaviness as we walked down the hallway. Although I sensed something was wrong, nothing prepared me for what I was about to hear. As tears welled up in her eyes, she explained that all my hard work was not enough.

Despite the many hours spent during study hall, after school, and before school, my economics teacher, Mr. B., wasn't satisfied with my work. After the bell rang, we went to his class to see what I could do to appease him. He didn't care if I walked with my class or not. I felt as if he were punishing me for the many days of class I missed. He didn't believe a student could complete the class without spending countless hours listening to his lectures.

Advocating for me, the guidance counselor tried everything to reason with him. She even suggested I walk with my class and receive an empty graduation folder until I completed summer school. Mr. B. offered no compromise, no compassion, and no care about all I was going through. He required his students to do certain things and expected them to do so. That was that.

The cold-hearted man dismissed us and prepared to teach his next class. I fell to my knees in tears. How could he do this? How could he take this from me? How can one teacher have so much control? With a heavy heart, I returned to the gym, where my classmates practiced the procession. I couldn't face them. I was in a nightmare, and everything was growing dim. The words became distant, and tears consumed my being.

I didn't understand how the last twelve years of hard work, good grades, and discipline could be overshadowed by this one class. How could this be real? All the years of hard work weren't enough for me to walk across the stage with my graduating class.

This disappointment of not graduating with my class did, however, reunite me with my family.

Lost in the moment and devastated by all that had happened, I called my parents to let them know I wouldn't be walking with my classmates. But Mr. Pickell offered some consolation: He invited me to sing with my class at graduation. We sang with mixed emotions and many tears. Kiara's parents sat on the front row of bleachers showing love and compassion toward us. We grieved their loss and ours.

I didn't graduate that day, but my parents, confident I would complete summer school and secure my degree, threw me a graduation party anyway. In addition to my family, friends and teachers came to show their love and support in what became a time of encouragement and healing. These were the people who believed in me and encouraged me to cross the finish line.

Summer school began the next week. I arrived early and sat in the front row for the first of many classes that summer. I never missed a day or an assignment. The defining moment came when I completed Mr. B.'s economics class. I'd worked hard for this moment.

I officially graduated from high school, but I was still haunted by the strains of "Pomp and Circumstance." That song was etched in my memory since watching my class walk across the stage and feeling separated from all the years we spent together. Alone in the moment I would never get back.

After completing summer school and receiving my diploma in the mail, I was invited to participate in the Class of '93 graduation ceremony. Although I knew the class as a whole, I didn't know them individually. I didn't want to celebrate with another class. Instead, I wanted to cry for all I'd lost since my car crash. My diploma reminded me of all I'd worked hard to achieve and all that had been taken from me.

CHAPTER 3

MENDING BROKEN PIECES

Despite all I was going through, I found hope when I attended Plymouth Wesleyan Church. Attending regularly and becoming a part of the choir filled those empty places in my heart and put the broken pieces of my life back together again. I'd found a church home.

I'll never forget the day Pastor Dave preached a sermon on Winnie the Pooh. Pastor Dave walked in with a plump stomach, grinning from ear to ear, and singing the theme song to the Disney movie. With a bounce in his step, he clicked his heels and continued to the stage, where he taught about God and His love for us.

Winnie the Pooh has intrigued, engaged, and even inspired both parents and kids for over ninety years. Pastor Dave shared how Winnie the Pooh and his friends reflect Jesus's love for us. They all remained faithful to each other despite their weaknesses. The anxious Piglet, depressed Eeyore, controlling Rabbit, bouncy Tigger, wandering Pooh, the wise but foolish Wol (owl), the migrant Kango and Roo, and the child, Christopher Robin, who faced many challenges growing up. All experienced the grace God offers each of us. Good news abounds in every season and challenge of life.

Pastor Dave ended the service with an invitation for all to encounter God's grace. God's grace flourishes no matter the challenges we face. At that moment, I knew Pastor Dave was talking to me. As I hastened to the altar with tears rolling down my face, I felt someone put a hand on my shoulder. A soft, feminine voice asked me if I knew Jesus. As she was praying, Pastor Dave walked up and prayed over me, asking Jesus to come into my life, erase all my past, and make me new again in Him.

Something happened to me that morning I could never explain. I was no longer a prisoner to my body and circumstances; I was made new in Christ and was filled with love and peace that would change my life forever. This was the love and peace I'd been searching for all my life. No one except my Lord and Savior, Jesus Christ, could provide it.

After we prayed, Pastor Dave invited me to a concert that night at the church with Sandi Jo. I didn't know who she was or what she sang, but I decided to go. That night, I walked into the church feeling like a new person. I sat in a pew toward the front of the sanctuary. Then the lights grew dim, and a spotlight followed a short, slender lady with long, curly, brown hair that bounced with each step she took to the center of the stage. I couldn't believe my eyes when I noticed it was the same sweet lady from that morning who'd laid her hand on my shoulder at the altar.

After a brief prayer, she sang, "What a Difference You Made in My Life." I felt like she was singing this song to me, and that she knew the difference God made in my life that morning. He made me whole again. He took all the broken pieces of my life that had been missing since the accident and glued them back together. Like a puzzle, He made a beautiful picture out of my brokenness.

But where would I go from here? I wanted to tell the world, as Sandi shared in her last song about the Great

Commission. I wanted to be a part of that. I wanted to be part of all God had for me.

The songs ministered to my heart in such a way that I found myself amid all that consumed me. A peace came over me as the tears ran down my face. I felt God wrap His arms around me as He carried me to the altar. Walking blindly in faith, I didn't know where to begin or how God could use someone like me. But I knew He was calling me. I also knew I wasn't perfect and certainly didn't have my life figured out, but I was willing to lay the pain and suffering I had endured at the foot of the cross.

As I knelt at the altar, I felt a gentle touch on my shoulder. The woman from the morning, and who had just done the concert, introduced herself as Sandi and prayed with me. I shared my story and testimony as I struggled to find my way. She invited me to her home for counseling and mentoring. She shared her testimony with me with a passion and love for Christ. Despite her husband's battle with cancer, they continued to minister together in music. Ed faithfully ran the sound at Sandi's concerts and prison fellowship gatherings. He had a heart of love and compassion with a charming personality.

Shortly after our counseling and mentoring sessions began, Ed was admitted to the hospital for surgery. Because the hospital was more than two hours away, Sandi needed someone to care for their precious dog, Maggie. I offered to do so and went to their house several times daily to feed and play with Maggie, eventually staying there while Sandi traveled back and forth. The days became long, and the nights grew dim as she traveled daily. We continued to pray for healing in this storm. We saw God's wonderful miraculous healing in Ed.

After Ed was released from the hospital, Sandi invited me to stay with them as I followed God's call to ministry.

Sandi introduced me to her alma mater—Indiana Wesleyan University (IWU), a faith-based college dedicated to helping students prepare for God's call on their life. Located in Marion, Indiana, IWU is an hour and a half from Ed and Sandi's home. They believed in me when I struggled to believe in myself. They also trusted God to work through my life.

Months spent going back and forth to campus, taking tests, filling out paperwork, and applying for financial aid were the beginning of a lifelong journey—one I never thought I could achieve and that I didn't feel worthy of following. Despite all the preparations, I knew in my heart I wouldn't be accepted. I continued to prepare myself for that letter which I assumed would be a rejection from the university.

Late one morning, Ed walked in from the mailbox carrying a large envelope from Indiana Wesleyan University. I remembered students saying that a large envelope from a college meant they were accepted. Could this be true?

Anxious and apprehensive, I opened the envelope and read President Barnes's letter congratulating me on my acceptance. I remember thinking this couldn't be true. Am I in a dream, or is this reality?

I continued to work during the summer and saved money to prepare for the fall semester of my first year at university. The days passed fast as we prepared for the next phase of my life.

One evening, I came home from work early to a room filled with ladies from the church who had generously bought things I needed for my college dorm. My heart was filled with love and joy as they all believed in me and God's calling on my life.

Getting accepted into IWU and becoming hall president were defining moments in this new chapter in my life. To reflect the new me, I began using my middle name, Ann.

While the name change didn't last long, it did keep Debra from connecting me with the girl she'd helped alongside the road four years before. Our paths crossed at my freshman orientation in 1995, where I introduced myself to Debra and her daughter as Ann. We connected several more times that year, either at church or on campus, but Debra didn't recognize me as the girl she laid in the back seat of her car and prayed over on that hot summer day in 1991. Her daughter and I attended classes together and took part in some of the same activities. Although my personality was outgoing, my real name was always hidden deep inside, as I searched for who I was.

Attending a Christian college was a pivotal period in my life. I spent long nights studying with friends and made many trips to Keystone and the Crossing Mall. Weekly chapel sessions continued to grow my faith and mend the broken pieces of my life. While all the chapel sessions played a profound part in helping my faith grow, one stands out.

On a cold, fall morning, students walked briskly across campus to attend chapel, piling into the warm building like every week before. Yet it was not at all like other weeks. An hour turned into days, and the days turned into a campus-wide revival.

The service began with a message of hope and ended with an invitation to leave our past behind. The worship team started the Rand Scruggs song, "Sanctuary (Lord Prepare Me)." Then they transitioned into "Jesus, Lover of My Soul." As students left their seats to go forward, we sang, "I surrender all; all to thee, my blessed Savior, I surrender all."

Not only did we surrender our hearts, but we also surrendered all the things holding us back. Students left and came back from their dorms with arms filled with things they wanted to leave at the altar, things they no longer wanted to hold on to, and things that divided them from their relationship with God.

The music continued for hours as students filled the altar with things they struggled to let go of. Addictions were broken, pasts were forgiven, and hearts were healed as tears flooded the altar. Many stayed at the altar for hours searching for their lost soul.

I was searching for the broken pieces of my life—the missing pieces from my childhood, my identity, my family, my senior year, and my faith. Jesus filled those empty holes as I surrendered everything to Him.

I left my past, my hurt, and my loneliness at the altar as I walked away in the wee hours of the next morning. I felt again like a new creation made alive in Christ. My life would never be the same. A peace flooded the campus like nothing I'd ever experienced.

Friends became like family as we lived in dorms together. Nights were filled with friends huddled together, studying.

But we didn't miss out on fun and laughter as we pranked each other, snuck guys into the dorm to hook up an answering machine, and even dressed one of the boys up like a little old lady to read us bedtime stories.

Sneaking out of the dorm past curfew to go to Walmart was a weekly adventure, along with warming up Pop-Tarts, popcorn, and other food on irons since we weren't allowed to have microwaves or hotplates in our rooms. Ramen noodles were a staple in every college student's diet. We never got into much trouble and enjoyed the time together. With no cell phones to distract us, we lived in the moment with our friends, sharing our passions, goals, and faith. We became a family in Christ, where I felt like I belonged.

Some classes were more challenging than others, but the teachers shared their faith and love for us. At this time,

FINDING FAITH IN THE STORM 27

I was a double major in psychology and social work. I loved the classes until I showed up to class and we were expected to touch a brain. Looking at the brain was fascinating, locating all the intricate details God used to create me. The psalmist's awe came to mind. "For you formed my inward parts; you knitted me together in my mother's womb. I praise you, for I am fearfully and wonderfully made" (Psalm 139:13–14).

While I was amazed at how the brain functions and enthralled to see it, my stomach wouldn't allow me to touch it. A pass-or-fail grade was on the line, however. I had no choice but to touch the slimy, squishy brain that lay before me. I tried to tell the instructor I couldn't do it. But she kept quoting, "I can do all things through him who strengthens me" (Philippians 4:13).

Yep, she was right. I could, but my stomach couldn't. Everything I ate for lunch came up and landed in front of me on the floor. At that moment, I knew the medical field was not the place for me.

I made lifelong friendships and continue to cherish many memories from my time on campus. Nothing in my life can ever replace the memories I missed out on that every child deserves to experience. Yet with the advances in social media and electronic devices, college will never be the same. Students are constantly connected but alone. Much of their time is spent on phones and other electronic devices connected to people around the world via social media. Yet while they're connected to so many they've never met in person. They are frequently alone among family and friends.

My faith continued to grow, and my dreams flourished as I completed my classes and was asked to be hall president. God had placed me on a path I felt I'd never expected and didn't think I was worthy of.

As the hall president, I spent many hours with the resident director planning a Big Sister/Little Sister induction ceremony for next year's incoming students. We wanted to create a sisterhood at Bowman Hall dorm. We wanted to ensure the girls felt a part of a family and not alone as they left all they knew behind to follow the path God had laid before them. Those cherished memories of college became a distant dream that summer.

CHAPTER 4

DWINDLING FAITH

I was sitting in the eastbound lane of a major intersection near the hospital in LaPorte, Indiana, when a fifteen-year-old boy barreled through the red light and broadsided me. The impact threw me into the dashboard, and my head crashed into the windshield. Glass shattered. Brakes screeched as vehicles ground to a halt.

Pain shot through my body. Sirens echoed in the air.

Flashbacks flooded my mind as the EMT loaded me onto the gurney. At the emergency room, I was awake when they began a series of tests and cleaned the blood from my head and body. Much of my pain came from the areas wounded in my accident five years earlier. Although the memories of that day had escaped my mind, the familiar, relentless pain returned.

I spent many months in and out of the hospital, followed by surgery and physical therapy. This time my body didn't heal as well or as quickly as the first time. Once again, I fought to regain my life.

Because I missed multiple classes due to treatments, returning to college became impossible. I didn't want to give in, but I knew I was losing ground again. My heart was filled with hopelessness, and my life was spinning out of control. I had no words. Lost in despair, I questioned if God was still there.

I was forced to withdraw from college. Eventually, I lost my grants and scholarships and realized I'd never return. Another chapter of my life had been stolen from me before it had started.

Tears flowed down my face as I packed my life belongings into suitcases and loaded them into the car. Memories of the past two years on campus flooded my mind: decorating our hall like the emerald city in the Wizard of Oz, all-night study sessions, winning the powder puff, sneaking out late at night to get ramen noodle soup from Walmart and cooking it on an iron, and sneaking guys into through dorm windows. Embossed amid those memories is the cherished memory of the Right to Life March in Washington, DC, and Homecoming. I'm grateful I got to experience those moments that I'll cherish for the rest of my life.

***

My car was packed full of all that once filled my college dorm. I turned off the light and locked the door as I exited for the last time. Walking down the hall, I felt like my life was over, like I'd failed at everything I'd ever tried to do. Tears flowed as friends gathered around me to say goodbye, and then I drove away. IWU became a vision in my rearview mirror. Another chapter of my life closed.

I returned home to face surgery and therapy. Pain consumed me. I no longer knew the words to pray. I depended on the Holy Spirit to go before the throne of God on my behalf. In my frustration, God reminded me, "'My grace is sufficient for you, for my power is made perfect in weakness.' Therefore, I will boast all the more gladly of my weaknesses, so that the power of Christ may rest upon me.

FINDING FAITH IN THE STORM 31

For the sake of Christ, then, I am content with weaknesses, insults, hardships, persecutions, and calamities. For when I am weak, then I am strong" (2 Corinthians 12:9–11).

We are to rejoice in our suffering, as painful as it is. Suffering strips away all distractions of life, forcing us to face our powerlessness. The fear of pain that goes with suffering draws us to the Father. Recognizing that we are powerless is the key to experiencing real power because we must become utterly dependent on God before His power can flow through our lives.

Jesus's disciples experienced two storms on the Sea of Galilee, much like the two major accidents I experienced. The Lord's purpose in both storms was to teach the disciples to stop relying on their physical sight and begin using their spiritual vision. Our physical eyes are blinded to the Holy Spirit. We must become blinded physically to truly see spiritually.

Feeling isolated and alone is one of the hardest parts of suffering. You feel abandoned by God and all those around you. No one knows what you're going through, nor do you want them to know. They would have to experience the pain and isolation you feel for them to understand. We're reminded of this in 2Corinthians, where Paul writes, "[God] comforts us in all our affliction, so that we may be able to comfort those who are in any affliction with the comfort with which we ourselves are comforted by God" (2 Corinthians 1:4).

I've learned the value of suffering. As a child of God, my pain is not pointless. Suffering not only develops compassion and mercy toward others but allows us to comfort others with the same comfort God has given to us. One of the most powerful words of encouragement I received was, "Your pain may not be about you. It may be preparing you to minister to others." This perspective brought me back to the question, "At what cost am I willing to be used?"

Am I willing to allow God's strength to shine through my weakness? God never wastes suffering. He redeems it all for His glory and our blessing. As I prepared for a new direction in my life, God reminded me "My grace is sufficient for you, for my power is made perfect in weakness." (2 Corinthians 12:8–9).

After leaving IWU, and eventually earning a degree in interior design, I traveled the Midwest setting up Hobby Lobbys. It was a dream job, staying in nice hotels and meeting new people. I spent my days decorating and my evenings with friends—often returning home on weekends to attend church and sing in the choir—my life had become whole again.

Mornings at home were spent watching the sun peek through the darkness of the cold, brisk mornings as squirrels hustled across the roof and birds sang their melodious songs. I knew they were a promise of a new day. Summer bids farewell as fall creeps in. Nature begins to die as winter approaches, preparing us for a new beginning. A day to sing of God's goodness and reflect on His promises that abound in His mercy.

Until one day in January 2005, I didn't know what the seasons of life meant. I suddenly became very ill and was no longer able to travel. My body began to fail me. My headaches became intolerable, and my body became numb as it began to convulse. I didn't know what was happening to me. I was scared and alone. I couldn't make it stop. I felt like I was locked inside a prison inside my own body, chained to walls of pain and despair.

My heart cries out in agony. Yet, no one hears me. With nowhere to escape, the pain consumes me and silences my heart's cry. I felt like a prisoner in my own body as I wrote this poem.

FINDING FAITH IN THE STORM 33

Imprisoned in My Body

Suddenly, I shake and twist so fast,
Never knowing how long it will last.
Convulsing like a rag doll,
I began to fall.
Arms flailing, legs kicking
to the sound of the clock ticking.
What is happening? I can hardly bear
As all those around me are in a silent stair.
Unable to stand.
To the floor, I will land.
My reputation it destroys
With a bone-crunching noise.
With my body mangled
and my arms and legs tangled,
I learned to rest in this place
As I seek God's loving face.
Imprisoned in my body today,
Not knowing the right words to pray.

    The hardest thing to do is trust God during a storm. For me, there was no relief from one storm before another hit. My body continued to quake. The doctors didn't know what was happening. One day, students joined the doctor on his rounds. After completing the exam, they stepped outside my door where I heard the doctor explain to the students that one day I may not escape all my body goes through. I'd been given a life sentence. I was diagnosed with a chronic illness that changed my life forever.

    Tears built up inside me. I could no longer deny the pain, and the doctors could not explain. Whatever was wrong with me was a mystery. Agony flowed with a vengeance through every cell of my body, seeking to conquer my mind and spirit. Pain became a knotted maze slicing through my core, haunting my soul with echoes of torment.

I endured many tests and procedures. My eyes were tired, and my body was growing weak. As I looked into the mirror one day, my reflection was different. I looked beyond what my eyes could see into my heart as I watched the medical team perform an echocardiogram. My muscles constricted with each heartbeat. The blood flowed gently like a stream through my veins. Watching how intricately our hearts work, I began appreciating God's beautiful craftsmanship. I am a masterpiece!

A few days later, I returned to the doctor. Diagnosis: no cure. Hope dwindled, and my faith grew weak. I felt abandoned by all. I continued working until the pain became too much to bear. My life, dreams, and body had drowned in the sea of pain. I had nowhere to turn and found myself in a cold, dark alley where God met me on my knees. Crying out in desperation I wrote these words

The Pain Consumes My Very Being

I can no longer fight this pain within me—
The pain that makes my head split,
A constant pressure that will not quit.
The thundering behind my eyes
Fills my head full of lies.
The pressure builds to a quake
That blinds me as I shake.
Everything starts to fade.
I no longer know the words to pray.
Pushing until it begins to break,
I now feel the pressure of an earthquake.
The light finds its way through,
Bringing me back to the God I once knew.

I felt like I was in a cave filled with anger and betrayal. I saw prisoners chained to the walls—prisoners of pain and abuse. The muddy floors pulled me in as I heard the groans of those within. They were trapped by the door of hopelessness. As I peeked through that door, a light peered from above. At that moment of despair, Jesus's light came "to give light to those who sit in darkness and in the shadow of death, to guide our feet into the way of peace" (Luke 1:79).

I heard the thunder roll in my footsteps. I saw the clouds cry. My heart felt the weight of the darkness, but my God cleared the way. He saw beyond my darkness and created a light that would shine in me, a ray of faith to guide my way. The storm may build, and the weight may become too heavy, but God has already prepared a place for me to stay safe during the storm.

Although the valley may seem dark and cold, beauty resides in the light that peeks through the clouds and illuminates the darkness. Each day is filled with bumps and curves, but I've learned to focus on the beauty surrounding me instead of on the pain that overtakes me. I've come to a place in my life where I'll fight for health. But I don't have to face my fears and health concerns alone. God is carrying me in the palm of His hand.

God never promises us an easy road, but He has promised to be at our side. "Come to me, all who labor and are heavy laden, and I will give you rest. Take my yoke upon you, and learn from me, for I am gentle and lowly in heart, and you will find rest for your soul" (Matthew 11:28–29).

That night, I accepted my cross and carried it. With the weight of the world on my heart, I walked down the dark alley to a hotel hidden by graffiti and trash. The room was dark, dingy, and dirty. With nowhere else to go, I spent hours cleaning. It reminded me of my life. When I first went to Jesus, my life was filled with darkness, pain, and sin, but He washed me clean from the inside out. We may fumble with the path we're on, but "If we confess our sins, He is faithful and just to forgive us our sins and to cleanse us from all unrighteousness" (1 John 1:9). With daily treatments and visits to the hospital, I could no longer afford the small, dark place I lived, and I had nowhere to go.

A lady from the church choir reached out to me with the love of Jesus. She invited me into her home and cared for me. She took me to my daily appointments for treatments and surgeries. The days turned into months. Now, eighteen years later, Donna Strite continues to care for me, never leaving my side, shining God's light into the darkest moments.

The day after I finished my treatments, Donna and I left for Florida. We stayed at my friend's home in Pinellas Park, Florida, for three months. Close to many beaches and lighthouses on the Gulf side, we spent time relaxing and recovering from all I had been through. We even experienced our first hurricane—Hurricane Wilma.

Having never experienced a hurricane, we heeded the warnings and boarded the windows and filled bags with sand. I made sure we had food and water—and a kite. Now we were ready for our hurricane party. We filled wine glasses with tea and toasted our friendship, then we flew my kite. Unfortunately, the kite-flying was not successful. The kite looked like a tornado whipping around in circles and tumbling to the ground.

Donna and I were curious about everything happening around us as the rain and wind picked up. Piling in the car, we drove down the road. I couldn't believe people were sitting outside eating at restaurants, and the stores were filled with people like any other day. While I was thinking about how crazy these people were, they probably felt the same about us driving around.

We stopped at Walmart, where we saw a father playing with his son. They wore superhero masks, and smiles caressed their faces—moments that will be cherished for a lifetime.

Hurricane Wilma arrived and did a great deal of damage to the surrounding areas. But God protected our tiny area, leaving us with little to no damage. The next morning, we ventured into the brisk, cold aftermath to try our kite-flying skills again. This time, the kite soared above the trees as we danced to keep warm. The beauty of the clouds was illuminated by the light of the warm sun, a stunning canvas painted by God's nature.

After warming up, Donna and I ventured to Madeira Beach. She dressed like an Eskimo while I was ready to surf the waves. The winds were brisk and the waves high. I had no idea what to do, but I knew I must try. The waves crashed violently against the shore as I ran into the freezing cold water carrying my dolphin boogie board. I didn't get very far before the waves carried me back to the beach.

This adventure ended before it began. My body was frozen with my hurricane "frozen, spiked hair." The wind blew sand in our faces as we hurried across the beach to our warm car. Entering the car, Donna was still trying to get the salt out of her mouth and off her body as she jokingly said it was the texture of sugar but tasted like dirt.

Each day in Florida brought precious memories along with pain. I became increasingly ill as the days passed, forcing us back to Indiana to begin treatment again. The trip home was long, and my mind was filled with anxious thoughts about the reality of my illness. I had nowhere to run and nowhere to hide and was running on empty. I was deceived by all that was around me.

The pain that consumed my life created darkness. Bits of light would break through as the chains became too heavy to bear. Visions of hope teased me as I was buried in pain and despair. I cried out for help. I cried out for someone to care. I was lost in a world of my own.

I got to live life for a bit, only to have it stolen from me. My famous words are, "I am OK!" because there are no other words to say. While searching for the right words to say, my life had become a blank page.

Blank Page

My life was filled with so many words to be read,
Then it became a blank page instead.
I would envision the words flowing across the sheet,
But the pencil and paper would never meet.
Colors around me had begun to fade
as I sat with a blank canvas and prayed.
My mind abandoned all that was true,
Looking for words it once knew.

Over the years, my hand would take me where my heart had been. The pages became my therapy, my refuge, and my best friend. Pages filled with secrets never told, lost in a world of the unknown. Soon, my pencil met the pages that held my darkest untold secrets. Like my life, the once vivid and clean pages are filled with darkness and soot.

Writing is a part of me; I get lost in the pages. When the words flow to the music of my heart, they transform into poetry on the page. My journal became my best friend as the words became my being sealed within the cover. As the years flowed by, my writing was no longer my secret hiding place. I was pouring my heart into essays at school, competing in Original Oratory on the speech team, and winning state competitions. I spent eighteen years of my life writing from the music of my heart. Today, my words are no longer my own but inspired by the greater One living in me.

CHAPTER 5

Peaceful Refuge

After three months in Florida, Donna and I returned to Indiana and looked for a place to call our own. We stayed in a hotel for several weeks, not knowing where to begin. As I glanced over the rental section of the local newspaper, an ad caught my eye. The ad read: a place in the country with rolling hills and beautiful landscape.

Sounded perfect. But it had to be too good to be true. With hesitation, I called the number.

Bev, the owner, was surprised to get our call because the ad was not supposed to run in the paper until the next day. With excitement, we asked to see the place that night.

We drove through miles of the countryside down winding, hilly roads. In the deep darkness of the night, I no longer knew where we were. Now, we were even more curious.

Finally, we made it to a duplex in the middle of nowhere surrounded by rolling countryside and a beautiful landscape, everything the ad described. We fell in love with the place the moment we walked through the door. We stood in a large, open-concept living-dining room with a four-seasons sunroom overlooking a peaceful pond in the backyard. The unit had two bedrooms and two baths with a large, finished basement, and a huge, cedar, walk-in closet. This was everything we ever dreamed of.

A week later, we moved in and met our neighbors, teachers from Ohio. Jack was onery, Jean loving. We spent many nights together playing games and baking. They brought joy into our lives, despite my pain. We built a friendship which I treasured.

Bev and her husband Bill never knew what they'd see when they drove past the duplex: monkeys in the trees, candy canes down the lane, or signs filled with love and friendship. Jack was always searching for ways to prank us with Jean at his side, and we'd retaliate out of love.

Jack and Jean became dear to us over the five years we lived there. They encouraged me as I learned to play the piano and loved me as I went for medical treatments. After four years, they told us they were moving out of the state to be closer to their family. I will never forget the long, white truck pulling up in front of the duplex as they loaded all their things. We were crushed as we watched them round the curve and drive away, taking with them a piece of our hearts.

Before long, Bill and Bev grew to be more than landlords to us and became our dearest friends who were like family. I spent countless hours in the sunroom practicing the piano. Our large deck looked down on rolling hills that cascaded down to the pond filled with fish.

We hosted themed parties with water slides, fishing, limbo, hula hoops, fireworks, and lots of joy and laughter with our friends and family. The years at the duplex gave me many precious memories I will always cherish.

Who would have known that a trip to see my ob-gyn would change my life forever? Over the years, I continued to have frequent pain that became more intense. The pain consumed my body, and I would lay in a fetal position in pain I could no longer bear.

After many unsuccessful procedures and treatments, surgery was the only option. What began as orthoscopic surgery ended with an incision from hip to hip after surgeons found a softball-sized tumor on my uterus along with an exorbitant number of uterine fibroids and much endometriosis.

After many days in the hospital, I returned home to find signs outlining our driveway telling me I was loved. My uncle Joe and aunt Phyllis were visiting my parents from California, and they visited the next day along with my auntie Mary. Despite the pain, my heart was warmed by their visit.

Auntie Mary played the piano as my uncle Joe sang in Czech. The words caressed the air as tears flowed down my mom's face. The scene captured moment that would remain embedded in their hearts. After the music faded, we sat around our round table with hot tea. We reminisced about their childhood and what my grandparents went through to immigrate from Czechoslovakia to the United States

Times have changed since then. To establish residency, my grandpa had to learn English, get a job, and buy a house before he could send for my grandma. Once he was established, he sent for my grandma, and they built a life here. I'm the second generation born in the United States. My aunt, uncle, and mom recalled my grandparents' struggles and triumphs. I recorded much of the day and cherish the videos even more since my uncle Joe and aunt Phyllis have gone home to be with the Lord.

My recovery grew longer and more difficult. My migraines became more severe and came more often. They went from one or two days a week to five or six days a week. Migraines often overtake your life. Some people consider them just a headache, but they are much more. They affect every part of your body. My head becomes lost in an illusion of a battle that has left me defeated. The migraine becomes an enemy with the intent to destroy my very being.

Defeated by the Migraine

Pounding louder than ever before,
I will not let her escape me anymore.
Pounding on her temples with my fists,
She knows I will not quit.
You cannot see the pain I cause.
As I create a whirlwind in her skull,
She falls like a boulder into her bed.
As I continue to pound on her head,
She cannot defeat me.
As the pain is more than anyone can see,
Pounding harder and harder
As her hope gets farther and farther.

As the migraines grew worse, I spent more time in the hospital. These trips became financially and physically burdensome, forcing us to move back to my hometown of Plymouth, Indiana, to be closer to my medical team. Donna and I looked for places in the area. Although we had no intention of moving yet, we happened upon a longtime friend in a subdivision who was preparing a duplex for rent. Pat had been Donna's beautician for years before retiring and was a member of the church I attended in high school and college. Neither of us had seen Pat for many years, and she and her sweet smile and warm hug welcomed us.

She welcomed us in, showed us the layout, and introduced us to her aunt Dona, who lived next door. Although Pat had a waitlist, she moved us to the top. Donna and I shared a knowing look. We realized God put us there at that moment and knew it was time to move again.

After twenty years of running from Plymouth to escape the memories of my past, I found myself running back to heal the present. My heart and mind were filled with mixed emotions. I knew this was where I needed to be but was reluctant to leave the place that had become our home—a refuge from all the pain. A place we had made our own.

We returned to our home in Warsaw that night with heavy hearts as we drove up the hill to Bill and Bev's house to give our thirty-day notice. Entering their home this time was different from the times before. We walked over to the long table and sat across from the two of them. With tears in our eyes, we told them we had to move at the end of the month. It felt like we were moving across the world and saying goodbye forever.

We weren't just moving; we were leaving family. Bev often brought her grandkids down the hill in her ATV. They loved to play Ping-Pong, basketball, and golf in our basement while the adults visited upstairs in the sunroom. The sunroom had special memories for Bev. Her mom had spent many hours reading her Bible here when she lived there. On hot days, we spent time in Bev's pool, up the hill. The countless hours spent together will always hold a special place in our hearts. Now, we began a journey down another road that diverged from this one.

After packing up the last of our stuff, we said goodbye to the place that had been home. We hugged each other with tearful eyes as Bev handed us an envelope. I opened the envelope while Donna drove down the winding road. Tears flowed down my face as I tried to read the words of love and friendship written inside the beautiful card. We were no longer friends. We'd become family who shared the memories of living in the duplex they built for her mother years ago.

Mixed emotions filled my heart as we left our life behind. The duplex in Plymouth was bright and beautiful, but much smaller. Although the walls were freshly painted, and the carpets clean, it was packed from corner to corner with all we owned.

Would we ever make this place our home? Would it ever feel like we belonged? Adjusting from two-thousand square feet to barely nine-hundred square feet was a challenge. We had to sell a lot of things and find places to store other possessions as we made our way through countless boxes. The days quickly filled with doctor's appointments, and all we had left became a distant memory as we created a new home.

Sunday after Sunday, we tried different churches. We were looking for one filled with the Holy Spirit and the love of God. Praying for God to lead and guide us, we were led to a church right around the corner from our new home.

One Sunday morning, we were awakened by the sun peeking through the clouds. I looked outside the window in awe of the beautiful things God has given to us. I was captivated by the beauty that comes from the darkness illuminated by the light. In the same way, our lives take both the light and the darkness to create such beauty. God gives us the canvas of our life to paint daily. Although some parts are painted for us, it's up to us to illuminate them with God's light.

Lost in my thoughts and prayers, I heard the birds chirping and squirrels hustling across the ceiling hours before the alarm sounded. Awakened earlier than planned, we decided to attend the second service instead of the third at Crossroads Church.

A greeter met us at the door with a smile and a bulletin. We headed to the left side of the sanctuary, where we noticed the drums in front of us. I'd had a migraine that morning, so we moved to the other side of the sanctuary. The rows filled with people as we headed toward the back of the church where a couple of open seats waited for us at the end of a row. We were getting comfortable when the pastor asked everyone to move to the middle of the pews to make room for more people to sit.

Donna and I moved to the center of the row and placed our Bibles on the seat as we turned to greet the people behind us. I greeted each of them with my name and a smile. But not until the end of the service did I understand God had put me at that exact place at that time.

At the end of the service, a short, brown-haired lady waited for us at the end of the pew. She had a warm smile and gentle eyes. In a quiet voice, she asked if she could ask me a question.

With curiosity in my voice, I said yes.

"Are you the same Pebbles who was in a car accident over twenty years ago on Hwy 17?"

"Yes, why do you ask?"

With tears of joy in her eyes, she said, "I was the one who found you on the side of the road and laid you in the back seat of my car when your car went into the ditch."

I could not believe what I was hearing. This was the lady who'd prayed over me as we waited for the ambulance to arrive. Tears flowed down my face as we embraced. I felt her gentle spirit and love, reminding me she was the angel God sent to protect me that day.

After many hugs and tears shed as we spoke of that day, her husband Larry shared his memory of Debra arriving home late that evening. "That accident changed her life," Larry said.

"I never forgot you," Debra said.

At that moment, God's light illuminated the darkness of my accident from over twenty years ago.

CHAPTER 6

THROUGH THE VALLEY

After meeting Debra, I reached another mountaintop but had to go through another valley. Alone, I was swallowed under by a current. My strength was no longer enough on its own. I cried out in pain and fear, asking my heavenly Father to hold me close. He carried me safely to the edge of the wave, where it anchored me until I could reach the peaceful shore. The waves were tamed, the storm was calmed, while faith carried me through yet another storm.

The storm built inside my head, and my migraines became worse than ever, affecting my memory and every aspect of my life. Looking for an escape, the valley became cold and dark. Every door I opened shut before I was able to enter. I cried out to God in pain and fear, not knowing where to turn. In and out of the hospital with no answers, no cure and no hope, the hospitalist referred me to Dr. Paula, a neurologist.

Dr. Paula wasn't like any other doctor I'd seen. She looked at me as an individual, not merely another migraine case. She wanted to help me as much as I needed her to give me relief. She ran multiple tests and tried many treatments, to no avail. She referred me to the best care facilities, only to discover that my insurance wouldn't cover them. My illness had taken hold of me with no hope of finding a cure.

I applied for clinical studies everywhere, hoping for a cure. I paid little attention to where the applications went. Then on May 8, 2013, I received an email from nurse practitioner (NP) LW at Johns Hopkins Hospital in Baltimore, Maryland. I replied with all the requested information, only to get a denial letter days later. My tiny bit of hope was once again crushed. My prayers became moments of despair, my nights darkened by pain, and my heart heavy and burdened.

I pleaded with God, not knowing where else to turn or what else to do. I was about to give up when I received a call from LW. After reviewing my thirty-page questionnaire, she knew I needed to be seen by one of their neurologists, but there were no openings. The first available appointment would be in January, almost a year away. Knowing I couldn't wait that long, she offered to see me herself a few weeks later.

Arlene, the pastor's wife from my childhood, was visiting family that week in Indiana. We had recently reconnected on Facebook and talked on the phone. Yet we hadn't seen each other in over thirty years. I was no longer the little girl she once knew. Not knowing what she would think of me, I became anxious as she approached our door. She greeted me with a hug that took me back to my childhood and the same gentle voice that caressed the air as she sang in the church we'd attended. As Donna and I prepared to travel to Johns Hopkins Hospital in Baltimore, she arranged to travel with us.

During the trip, we reminisced about many fond memories of bonfires near their barn and singing around the campfire. I was taken back to my childhood when I was only five. We laughed and cried as we shared heartfelt memories.

About halfway to Johns Hopkins, my pain overwhelmed me. I wanted to say I was OK. But I wasn't. I didn't know what was happening to me or why. The fear and pain overcame me as tears cascaded down my cheeks. My eyes blurred as moments were filled with total darkness. The pain assailed my body, my thoughts, and my life.

I was learning to lean on Jesus. Second Corinthians tells us that in our weakness, He is made strong. I continued to grow as my faith was tested daily. God never promised an easy road, but He has promised to be at my side. I believed He was there, but I didn't understand why He wouldn't take this pain from me. Why did He allow me to suffer?

When we arrived at Johns Hopkins, much of my time was spent on tests, procedures, and infusions. The remaining time was spent in bed at the hotel. I had barely enough strength to face another day.

Day after day, we traveled back and forth to the hospital. The days became long and wearisome. From the large window in our hotel room, all we could see was Johns Hopkins.

I don't know what came over me, but I couldn't stop crying. My emotions overwhelmed me; I feared what they might find as well as what they might not. I hoped for a cure yet feared doctors would not find one. Fear, pain, hope all bubbled inside and overflowed through tears.

After settling into the hotel after my first appointment, we went to see the Seven Foot Knoll Lighthouse. It sat alone on the shore, isolated from everything around. I felt much the same way—alone, isolated. The lighthouse brought hope to me in my suffering. The tall, round, red building with its huge beacon guiding the ships ashore reminded me that Jesus is my lighthouse. I wouldn't be where I am today without Him. I'd be lost in an ocean of darkness and despair.

The following day, we prepared to see LW for the results of my many tests and procedures. As we waited for the shuttle to the hospital, anxiety built inside me. Once on the shuttle, each additional stop seemed like hours. We reached the campus and headed toward the Bayview Medical Building, where I waited in line and prepared for the worst.

I couldn't take any more disappointment. I didn't know how much more I could bear. The waiting room was filled with people from around the world waiting with fear and pain in their eyes. No one spoke to each other. They kept their eyes directed toward their phones, iPads, and books.

Hours passed as we waited in a dark corner of the waiting room, isolated from all around us, when finally, a young girl opened the door and called out my name. I slowly walked toward her wearing sunglasses to shade the brightness of the long hallway. She guided me to a small room at the back of the building.

I sat in that room with anticipation and fear building inside me until LW walked in with a peaceful smile. She didn't have all the answers, nor did she pretend to. She knew I had a long road ahead of me, but she gave me hope for the journey. LW tried to ease my fear and pain and prescribed new medications and prepared me for several upcoming appointments the following week. She gave me a bit of light in my darkness.

As we were leaving the appointment to go to Arlene's house, a migraine attacked me like a lion, leaving me lifeless. The right side of my body became paralyzed, and my eyesight blurred. At the hotel, Donna did all she knew to do while Arlene watched in fear of what might happen next.

I try to live a life that glorifies God daily, shining His light for others to see. Like the song "This little light of mine, I am going to let it shine," I want His light to shine in me no matter what I face. Although Satan tries to blow it out, I must remind myself that God is more powerful and lives in me. Not by my strength but by His. That's how I'm able to face another day.

We had planned on taking Arlene home, but because I'd become so sick, her son Brian picked her up the next morning and headed home. My tears bubbled over as I faced another day of emotional soup. Shortly after Brian arrived, we left for home, emotionally, mentally, and physically exhausted by the trip.

Over the next several weeks, my migraine continued to build to the point where it never quit. I didn't have a day without it. While some days I was able to function despite the fog and pain, other days knocked me to the ground where I couldn't even pray. The new meds attacked my body from the inside out. The medications kept me in a mental fog where I didn't know where I was or what I was doing. I was no longer living but merely surviving. Unable to keep food down, I learned the medications were damaging my stomach and colon. When I had to go off the medicine and start over again, I had moments of complete blindness as everything became dark around me

On July 23, 2013, I woke up at two a.m. with a migraine that blinded me in my right eye and left me motionless. My ophthalmologist got me into his office right away. Over the course of two hours, he ran several tests. As I sat in front of a large, round cave filled with little dots that blinked on and off, puffs of air measured the pressure in my eyes and revealed swelling of my optic nerve and a narrowed vision field.

He contacted Johns Hopkins Hospital to set me up with a neuro-ophthalmologist for the next day. He also sent a report to LW at Johns Hopkins because he was concerned the optic nerve swelling might be associated with the pressure in my head that wouldn't go away. The pressure continued to pound along with a whooshing of water in my ears.

We left home to head back to Johns Hopkins.

My NP at Johns Hopkins set me up to see one of the neurologists who specializes in intracranial pressure. He ordered a lumbar puncture the same day. Things were moving fast; my head was overwhelmed, and my emotions consumed me. I felt like I was on a train that kept going faster, had reached a cliff, and was about to go over.

The medical personnel prepared me for the lumbar puncture in a cold, dark room. Lying on a hard cot with a hospital gown and a blanket didn't keep me warm as they rubbed cold, local anesthetic to clean and numb the area.

Then the neurologist came in and explained the procedure to me. He inserted a long needle between two bones in my lower back to enter my spine in the lumbar region. He reminded me not to move as he continued to move the needle to find the right location to measure the pressure while spinal fluid flowed out of me through the needle in the curvature of my spine. I was afraid to breathe. Afraid to move. Then suddenly, he hit the wrong spot, I jerked, sending a shock of pain down my right leg. My body trembled.

"We are in," he said. He continued to speak to me in a gentle voice as he saw the tears flow down my cheeks.

Time passed slowly as I lay in the same position for over an hour. My hip hurt, and my back spasmed as the fluid slowly drained into the large glass tube. About midway into the draining, my sight became more vivid. Everything around me was no longer dark and dim. I had instant relief from the pressure in my head. The pounding in my head and the whooshing in my ears had stopped. I finally felt relief. I finally felt like I would be OK! I finally felt hope again.

At the end of the procedure, the doctor left as the nurse cleaned my back and helped me get dressed. Donna sat at my side, praying as we waited for words of hope and encouragement.

When the doctor entered the room, he said, "I have good news and bad news. The good news is we discovered what's causing the pressure. The bad news is there is no cure." He went on to explain pseudotumor cerebri, also known as idiopathic intracranial hypertension, that appears when the pressure inside the skull increases for no clear reason. The symptoms mimic a brain tumor. The increased pressure can cause swelling of the optic nerve, resulting in vision disturbances or loss. A lumbar puncture drains the fluid and releases the pressure, often giving instant relief.

The neurologist explained the different treatment options, including medications and possible surgery to insert a shunt. With my history of autoimmune and allergic reactions to many medications and procedures, we opted to try the least invasive medication and lumbar punctures to drain the fluid. Medications are not always enough to reduce the pressure and the headache, but with regular lumbar punctures, the patient often feels relief.

He started me on a medication that caused hallucinations and hives. It put me in the ER at Johns Hopkins Bayview. They took me off the medication at once and began a Benadryl IV drip. The next day, he changed the medication and observed me for the next twenty-four hours. I continue with the same treatment today along with regular draining.

After the lumbar puncture, they didn't want me to travel home right away because the hole in my spine where they drained the fluid needed to clot, creating a plug that wouldn't allow the spinal fluid to leak.

I laid flat without a pillow for over an hour to ensure it healed. With such a long trip home, that night we went to Arlene's home in Virginia Beach for me to have time to recover. In the middle of the night, I woke up with a pain in my head that consumed every fiber of my being every time I sat up. The room started spinning, and I got dizzy and felt like I was going to pass out. What was happening? Hope was fading, and fear took over as the pain rose.

Arlene and Donna took me to Sentara Hospital in Virginia Beach. Before long, a doctor came in and said I was experiencing a spinal headache and needed an epidural blood patch where they injected blood from my arm into the same epidural space to stop the cerebrospinal fluid leak. The pressure became unbearable as they forced the blood into a tiny opening to create a clot to prevent the fluid from leaking. After many attempts, they finally got the blood into the space needed. They rotated me to lie on my back for hours, allowing the opening to clot.

This was not how I wanted to start my first visit to Virginia Beach. The blood patch helped my head instantly. Over the next couple days, I began to heal and was able to go to the beach, where all my pain and fear faded with the sun on the horizon. The waves crashed against the shore, and the sand melted between my toes as I walked across the sand.

Walking along the shore alone with my thoughts took me to a spiritual place where I experienced God and my faith in a new and closer way. The silence of the air brought peace over me as the caressing waves sang to me. The smell of salt cleansed me, and God's presence consumed me. Watching my footprints wash away with the currents, I was reminded that God was carrying me. The ocean became my peaceful refuge, representing the many storms of my life.

The Ocean

I feel the violent waves crashing against me.
Each time I try to rise above, I am swallowed by
an undercurrent.
The same ocean where I feel my peaceful refuge
is now a roaring sea.

> My heart beats so heavily, and my body is filled with so much pain.
> The serenity of the crashing waves is now raging against me.
> The vicious thunder and lightning overtake my cries.
> My body was beaten, tired, and worn, feeling the tide about to take me again.
> Alone, the waves swallow me under, with no strength left anymore.
> Then my heavenly Father carries me safely to the shore
> Where the waves are tamed and the storm is calmed once more.
> My faith carries me through another storm.

I felt my faith fading away, lost in the riptide of my pain. That's when Jesus took me in His arms and brought me to His peaceful refuge as I made a new commitment to turn my life over to Him. At that moment, I knew I wanted something more. I knew I wanted to share my faith despite my pain and suffering. I wanted to make an outward display of my faith by being baptized in the ocean, where I'd found God once again. Despite ongoing pain, trials, and travel, I continue to seek Him. Sometimes I get lost along the way, but He always guides me back to where I'm meant to be.

The morning at Arlene and Dan's house, we prepared to go to church, where we met many people, including prayer warriors who'd been praying for me and believing in a miracle for me. They greeted me with smiles and hugs as the worship began, followed by a time of prayer and a powerful message of faith and healing. The Holy Spirit met me in that place. Seated beside Arlene, childhood memories returned, and I felt like the little girl of thirty years ago.

After the service, we made our way to the car, talking to many people who shared their love and prayers.

Knowing my passion and love for horses, Arlene and Dan took Donna and me to the Lynnhaven Mall in Virginia Beach, where there was a two-story carousel in the middle of the large, glass room. Once again, I stood like a little girl in awe of this carousel's beauty, the exquisite craftsmanship, the pastel colors, and the intricate details of each painted horse. The horses slid up and down the gold-painted bars as the organ music filled the air. I wanted nothing more than to ride one of the beautiful masterpieces.

As I approached the long line of children, Arlene's husband Dan offered to ride with me—a moment I'll never forget as we loaded onto the second level. I chose a beautiful white horse with a flowing main and tail, and he chose the horse next to me. We rode into the sunset together (OK, so I imagined riding into the sunset). But I felt the freedom of being on a horse. The freedom of escaping all I'd endured that week. I was alone with God in the moment.

The ride ended. I bid the horse goodbye and walked to the exit to meet Arlene and Donna. We left the horses and headed to the food court. The smells filled the air from restaurants that lined the area. Picking one was difficult because they all looked and smelled enticing. We each chose something different and then shared our meals. After a long day, we returned to Arlene and Dan's home, where Donna laid down for a nap.

While Donna peacefully slept upstairs, my pain kept me awake. As I rested on the couch, Arlene and I took a trip down memory lane.

As a child, my family lived in the old parsonage next door to the church. I was about four years old when I first entered those big, white doors to the church and walked down the long aisle to where Arlene sat. She introduced herself as the pastor's wife and invited me to sit next to her. This was the beginning of a lifelong relationship.

Our families spent countless hours together during the week. We went to their house, where Arlene would watch us while my mom worked. We ventured into the old barn, played games with the children outside, and sang songs around the bonfire. When we weren't at their house, their kids loved coming to our house, and we often went back and forth between the two homes during the week and to church on Sundays.

This continued until they moved out of the state. God called Dan to ministry in Virginia Beach, where he went to school and got his doctorate in ministry. We often wondered what had happened to them and if we'd ever see them again. Thirty years later, we were reunited on social media.

During the week we spent with them, the beach was my refuge. It became my secret hiding place, where I found God amid all my pain and suffering. He carried me through the storms and brought me safely to the shore, where I found a renewed strength in Him. Excited about what God had done in my life, I wanted to make an outward sign of my commitment to trust and follow Him. "I want to be baptized in the ocean," I said. "That's where I've found God in the storms of my life—it's my sacred hiding place."

Dan and Arlene reached out to Marlon, the pastor of their church, and his wife, Bobbie Jo, who wanted to share in what God was doing in my life.

They picked a day and time that worked for everyone to meet at Virginia Beach. When we arrived at a private part of the beach, we were alone in the quiet of the morning. We walked across the wooden steps to reach the white sand as a cool breeze caressed our faces, the sun illuminated the water, and the taste of salt permeated the air.

The presence of the Holy Spirit filled this place as we gathered in a circle to pray and share in the meaning of baptism. With waves lapping, birds singing, and the sun shining in the crisp morning breeze Marlon read from his Bible:

Peter reminds us, "Repent and be baptized every one of you in the name of Jesus Christ for the forgiveness of your sins, and you will receive the gift of the Holy Spirit" (Acts 2:38).

After he read the Scripture, we walked down the beach into the ocean, where the waves crashed over my head as if the Holy Spirit were baptizing me along the way. Pastor Dan and Pastor Marlon were ready to baptize me. They stood on either side of me as the water now reached above my waist.

I covered my nose as they laid me back. "In the name of the Father, Son, and Holy Ghost," they baptized me, and the moment I went down, a wave came and brought me back to my feet.

The others cheered as we walked back to shore. The Holy Spirit filled me with His love and peace, and I felt a fullness of joy and happiness I hadn't felt before. On that day, I was united with Christ in a new way. My faith was stronger than it had ever been. I was washed clean from the dark spots of my past and shining like the newness of white snow.

That week passed quickly, and we returned to church before returning to Johns Hopkins Hospital. I felt the pressure of what was to come, and fear threatened to overtake me as we prepared to leave after the service.

Arlene had packed to go with us and waited at the hotel as I went for more tests. I had to spend the night in the hospital hooked up to lots of wires and leads as they watched my brain activity while I slept. Yet all the wires and leads made it impossible to sleep. I tossed and turned, pulling on the wires with each move and setting off alarms—I accidentally pulled them off. Although they were able to monitor me closely, sleep never came. I had to be up and ready to leave that building at five a.m. to arrive at six a.m. for my MRI and MRA at another building.

I was exhausted when they finished everything in the wee hours of the morning. We returned to the hotel where Arlene had been sleeping peacefully. She was surprised by our early morning return. The hardest part came after the tests, waiting for the results before I could return home.

The hotel room became a holding place. A place where we spent countless hours waiting for the next procedure and even more hours waiting for the results. With what little energy we had left, we decided to escape from the captivity of the hotel. With my phone in hand, we headed to Fort McHenry and the Cheesecake Factory as we awaited the results of my tests and the clearance to go home.

When we finally returned to the hotel, I dozed off but was awakened by the call we'd been waiting for. I was scheduled to meet with a neurologist at eight o'clock the next morning. We packed everything and loaded it into the car to be ready to leave after my appointment the following day. Leaving the hotel in the morning darkness was symbolic of the darkness that filled me with fear of what the doctor would say or do.

I entered the patient room with hopes for the answers and a cure for my illness. Although LW, the nurse practitioner, didn't have either, she gave me a bit of hope along with more uncertainty.

As we prepared to leave her office, she asked us to wait to leave town until she received the rest of the results. Discouraged, we headed back to the hotel. We were exhausted and napped until two p.m. when we received the call I'd been waiting for.

The doctors confirmed the previous diagnosis after reviewing the final test results. My final confirmed diagnosis was pseudotumor cerebri. Pseudotumor cerebri is elevated cerebrospinal fluid in the brain causing pressure that mimics a brain tumor. Symptoms include headaches and blurred vision, which can develop into permanent vision loss. I will never forget the words, "There is no cure." The words kept echoing in my ears as we drove back to the beach. Looking across the miles and miles of water, I saw the waves lapping.

As the tide gently cascaded to the shore, a fierce wind came from nowhere and caught me, throwing me back into the storm once more. The sky turned dark as midnight. The ocean was rigid with riptides pounding against the shore. The sky lit up with bolts of lightning and loud echoes of thunder.

I was all alone while tears flowed endlessly down my face, crashing on the ocean floor. But as the sky began to quake, a sense of peace filled the air and calmed the storm. I was alone but was now resting in my Father's arms.

CHAPTER 7

LEARNING TO LEAN

After such a dreaded diagnosis, I didn't know what was ahead of me, nor was I prepared for what happened next. My eyes were tired, and my head was filled with pain when we returned to Arlene's. That night, sharp stomach pains assaulted me with every breath. Fear consumed me. Arlene and Donna rushed me to the hospital, where I was taken straight back to the examination room. The staff ran numerous tests before calling a surgeon. Then they transferred me to a clinical observation room while we waited for the surgeon to arrive.

In the observation room, Arlene and Donna rested on comfortable furniture. Soon, however, Arlene called Dan to pick her up. As Donna and I waited for the surgeon, my pain grew more intense. After reviewing the tests, the surgeon came in and explained that my lower abdominal hernia was entrapped in my stomach wall, requiring immediate surgery. Not knowing what to expect when he got into my abdomen, he explained that he planned to go into my stomach arthroscopically. Still, he might have to convert to open surgery if needed. Seeing few other options and uncertain what to expect, I agreed.

Shortly after the surgeon left, Donna called Arlene with the news. Not long after that, Arlene returned to the hospital. She walked in as they were wheeling me down the hall at about five p.m. for what was supposed to be a two-hour surgery.

Three hours passed with no update; four hours passed, and no one was in sight. The waiting room was dark, with a small light in the corner as they awaited news. Arlene couldn't stay awake anymore and called Dan to take her home, leaving Donna alone—tired and waiting. With no sleep from the night before, her eyes grew weary as the hours passed. Becoming increasingly concerned, she went down the hall to find a nurse who called surgery.

"The surgeon's run into many complications," came back the response. "Surgery will last another two hours or more." With a sense of relief and concern and heavy eyelids, she dozed off in the wee hours of the morning.

Hours later, the surgeon found Donna in the waiting room and explained surgery had been much more invasive than he'd planned. He found several hernias entrapped when he placed the camera into the abdominal wall, forcing a quadruple hernia repair with staples reaching from the top of my stomach to the bottom. Before he left the waiting room, he added, "She may never stand up straight again because the extensive repairs pulled the abdominal muscles so tight."

Arriving back to my hospital room in the middle of the night, the nurses prepared to transition me from the gurney to the bed. I was stubborn. Despite the pain, I insisted on walking the hall before lying down in bed. The nurses looked at each other in shock. "We'd better check with the doctor." To their surprise, I walked the whole floor before lying down.

My body was covered with wires, an IV, and an abdominal binder wrapped so tightly moving was difficult. Each breath was painful. No matter which way I turned, the bed became my worst enemy. It hurt to sit up. It hurt to lie down. I couldn't take the pain anymore. At three a.m., I wanted nothing more than to go for a long walk around the entire floor. I wanted to do anything but lie in that hard, uncomfortable bed. The nurse came and walked me repeatedly throughout the night.

While the halls were peaceful and quiet throughout the night, no one told me I was mooning everyone with each step I took. (Aren't the nurses supposed to make sure we're completely covered when we're on a pain pump and don't know what we are doing?). Thank goodness it was three in the morning, and most people were in bed fast asleep.

Arlene didn't rise to the occasion as I stood up straight and walked the halls. But Donna, camera in hand, caught it all, even my full moon—without even noticing. I was grateful for the delete button.

Thanks to my pain pump, the first day went better than expected. I spent many hours walking the hall with a gown to cover my backside. I began to think this wasn't too bad. I could handle this one moment at a time. Between walks, I dozed off. When the doctor came by, he was amazed at how well I was doing. "But," he warned, "the local anesthetic hasn't worn off yet." Boy, was he right!

Day two was a different story. When the local anesthesia worn off, the pain consumed me to my core. People from the church visited me. My room filled with gifts and flowers of love and prayers. But no matter what I did, the pain was too much to bear. I wanted nothing more than for the pain to stop and to go home to Arlene and Dan's house to recover.

After several days, my pain began to get under control. I was released to go to my home away from home. The bedrooms in Arlene and Dan's were upstairs. I knew I could never reach the top of the stairway. Arlene pulled out a hide-a-bed in the family room for me. I had to bend to reach the edge. As I did so, I felt every staple in my stomach pull. I struggled to lower myself to the two-inch mattress. Once there, the springs pressed into my back. Why had I been so eager to be released from the hospital? Even the hard uncomfortable bed there would have been better than this.

The hours passed slowly as I twisted and turned, trying to find a comfortable spot with the rough springs. I missed having a nurse to respond to my needs. Here, I had no button to summon assistance and no money to get the pain pills the doctor had prescribed. I kept telling myself, "You can do this," But no matter how many times I said it, the pain made it impossible to believe.

A friend mailed my pain medications from home, but it took two of the longest days of my life to receive them while waiting for relief. I couldn't lie down, and I couldn't sit up. Sitting caused the staples to pull, and lying down caused them to stretch.

The pain medication took longer than expected and arrived a couple days before we were to make the dreaded trip back to Indiana.

The following day, we prepared to go to church. With a strong message about faith, the service ended with the song "Learning to Lean," which reminded me that our faith is a constant work. I'm learning to lean more on Jesus. People will always fail us, but Jesus will always be there to catch us when we fall. My faith grew again as I was reminded of God's faithfulness.

We left the church with lots of hugs and prayers. Saying goodbye to everyone was like leaving family behind—my family in Christ. I was exhausted when we got home. I laid down to take a nap, looking forward to the next day when the staples would be removed. They hurt so much and had become embedded into my belly button. I felt like they would rip out as they would catch onto each other and pull.

We left early the next morning, only to arrive at the wrong hospital to see the surgeon. With directions to the hospital where we'd find the surgeon, we drove to the right hospital. My anticipation to have the painful staples removed grew by the moment.

Finally, the nurse took me back to the room where I got more dreaded news. The surgeon took one look at the incision and said, "It's not completely healed; the staples cannot come out yet."

That was the last thing I expected or wanted to hear, and I cried. This couldn't be real. We were packed and ready to leave Virginia the next morning. I couldn't believe this was happening.

I'd have to go another week with over sixty staples that pulled and tugged on my skin with every step, every movement. I wanted to go home. As the tears flowed down my cheeks, the surgeon offered me a tissue. "Tell me what you're feeling."

I could not speak. Emotions flooded my mind. Donna spoke for me. "We were prepared to go home."

He placed his hand on my shoulder. "I want to help. I wish I could ease your pain. Traveling will be painful, but I know how important it is to you to go home." Reluctantly, he decided to let me go if my family doctor agreed to remove my staples in a week. We called her, and without hesitation, she agreed.

Arriving back at Arlene's, I told her the surgeon had not removed the staples. She thought I was kidding until I showed them to her. Her heart broke for me because she knew how much pain they caused. To ease the pain, we went for a short walk on the beach, even though storm clouds threatened. We watched closely as the storm passed by. Even in the clouds, I saw the beauty within, as a tiny light peeked through. No matter how dark things may get, God's light shines the brightest when life looks the darkest.

As the hours passed by that night and we got closer to leaving, I began pulling away, something I've learned to do to ease the pain of saying goodbye. We finished packing and got ready for bed, preparing to leave in the wee hours of the morning before Arlene usually got up. The night went by slowly. I woke every hour on the hour as I continued to hide my feelings deep inside. Feelings that I didn't know I had, feelings that protected me from that much-dreaded word. *Goodbye.*

Arlene made breakfast for us, and Dan prayed with us as we were ready to walk out the door. Each bump in the road felt like someone was tugging on one of the sharp staples in my stomach. Jolting me from one side to the next, I felt the staples in my belly button catch on to the other and pull. It felt like the staples were ripping out.

Just when I didn't think anything else could go wrong, the car began to shake. Something was wrong. We were too far to turn around and too far to make it home. I found a repair shop and pulled over. We had a nail in our tire. We endured more waiting for a tow truck.

At the repair shop, we sat on hard, plastic chairs for three more hours. What was I thinking? Why didn't we wait to make this trip? The tears let loose like a tsunami. Why can't I control these tears? Ever since the surgery, they seem to overtake me at a whim. These past two weeks, I've cried an ocean of tears that continue to flood my heart.

With the tire repaired, I was determined to drive to Ohio before stopping for a hotel room. We were both exhausted as we crossed over the line into Youngstown, Ohio, and got a room at the Hampton Inn.

The manager asked why we were traveling, and after sharing with her, she gave us our room for free. "I hope that relieves some of your stress. Sleep as long as you need to," she said. This was another reminder that God is always there, supplying our every need.

The following morning, the manager shared that her daughter had recently passed away from cancer. "You've inspired me," she said, "in the midst of my grief." I've since noticed that God often supplies our needs while using us to minister to others in ways we may never know.

The next morning, I woke to the most wonderful surprise—a call from my three-year-old niece. "I'm peeling apples with Grandpa. We're making an apple pie." Without stopping for a breath, she went on to tell me about her new purse and shoes that Grandma got her. My heart was warmed as I smiled nonstop.

Then she finished with, "And Aunt Pebbles, I miss you." Hearing that was the best medicine I could've ever received.

We finally got on the road, left Ohio, and entered Indiana, arriving early in the evening. We didn't even unpack our car before surprising my brother and his family. We were greeted with big hugs. My niece and nephew were excited to see us as they shared all they did over the past month. They are the joy of my heart. I'm blessed with a wonderful brother and sister-in-law who share their children with me. They all are lights in the storms of my life.

Exhausted from the trip and still in pain with a stomach full of staples, we didn't stay long. We made a quick stop at my parents before heading home. I was grateful to be home and surrounded by a loving family, but I longed for my soft bed. There, I spent most of the next several days, recouping from the trip.

I hadn't completely recovered from the latest surgery before getting that dreaded call from Johns Hopkins saying

I had to return in a few weeks. I barely had time enough to get my stitches out, unpack to repack, and go again. This was the start of many trips to Johns Hopkins Hospital and less time at home.

At the beginning of this journey, my family, friends, and church showered me with support. They were there to lift me up when I didn't have the strength to stand on my own. But as the days and months went by, I heard from them less often. I felt alone and like I couldn't go on. We were growing deeper and deeper in debt as the trips multiplied. The doctors in Indiana could do no more for me, but I didn't have enough money to continue traveling to Johns Hopkins. I felt like I was drowning in an ocean, and there wasn't anyone to save me.

I was reminded of the song we sang at church in Virginia, "Learning to Lean." Every day, I was learning to lean on Jesus. I knew I wouldn't get through whatever lay ahead in my own strength, but only by the power of God. I learned that faith isn't about being strong, but about being weak so that God can be strong in me. God wants to be number one in our lives. He wants to be above all things. No matter how tough things are, He will supply all our needs if we put our trust and faith in Him. "God will supply every need of yours according to his riches in glory in Christ Jesus" (Phil 4:19).

Donna ended up with bronchitis and pneumonia a few days before we were to return to Johns Hopkins Hospital. Arlene flew into Indianapolis to make the trip with us. She spent a couple days with us before we left. The next morning, we all slept in until almost noon after such a late night.

I couldn't believe the time, and we had so much to do to get ready to leave, and my brother Ron was coming to visit that night. Ron arrived at six o'clock. I hadn't seen him for over ten months, which seemed like a lifetime. We reminisced about our childhood spent at Arlene and Dan's house. The memories of singing around the bonfire, playing in the barn, and the schoolhouse as it was being built. Like the song "Precious Memories," precious memories flooded our hearts and souls. After over four hours of reminiscing, the time was late, and we were sad to see Ron go home.

Exhausted, I laid my head on the pillow as memories of my past and present entered my mind. Some I'd hidden deep in my heart where no one could find them. I remembered the morning I awoke after being raped at a friend's house and later at the hospital when I miscarried my baby girl. These are memories I haven't shared with many. No one could understand what I went through. Memories that will always leave tiny footprints on my heart of a little girl who I carried on this earth for just a moment. She was taken from me before I even got to hold her in my arms. Although I never held her, she will always be in my heart. During this time of suffering and pain, God called me to come to the well.

Come to the Well

I suffered so much loss on that day.
There were no words that I could pray.
I was drowning in an ocean of tears.
Wanting to hold my baby girl near
As I struggle to take each breath.
I am reminded of your untimely death.
I've heard of this place to go
To find the answers I need to know,
Hidden within a garden of care
Where the Father is always there.
He is the one I have been searching for
In hopes of finding peace to fill my heart once more.
He said to come to the well, where I would search no more.

Standing there, hoping to hold on even more,
I asked Him to bring you back to me, with no reply.
I knew it was time to say goodbye.
With so much sorrow, I began to walk away
When I heard Jesus say,
"I am the resurrection and the life.
The one who believes in me will live, even though they die.
And whoever lives by believing in me will never die.
Do you believe this?" (John11:25–26).

My pillow was drowned in tears, and my heart was shattered in pieces as I remembered that day like yesterday. I finally fell asleep in the darkness of the night and woke to the dawn of another day.

The following day, we visited the sight of my accident in 1991—the day that changed my life forever. Until then, I'd always avoided that road due to my fear of reliving that day. We parked next to the curve that once was filled with ambulances and police cars. I walked anxiously to the edge of the road. I saw where my body once lay and the deep, dark hole where my car landed.

Looking back, I remember everything clearly as my life flashed before my eyes. I don't know how I escaped that accident. I don't know how I reached that hilltop. Memories flooded my mind as the pain still invaded my body. I don't understand why God allows so much suffering. Yet through my grief and pain my faith continues to grow.

That night, I struggled to fall asleep. Visions from that day of flashing lights and sirens screaming overpowered my mind. I tried to envision what my life would be like if that accident had never happened. I became overwhelmed by my thoughts and couldn't fall asleep. In the wee hours of the morning, I finally drifted to sleep.

Waking up later than planned, we packed our stuff into the car and headed toward the curvy mountains of West

Virginia. The smell of fall welcomed us as we rounded the mountains bursting with trees covered in yellow, orange, and red leaves. The cold, brisk air reminded me summer was gone and winter was waiting to greet us. We traveled alongside the mountain as we marveled at the beautiful landscape God had painted for us.

Arriving back at Arlene's house early that evening, we didn't let the raindrops stop us from going to the beach. As we walked along the water in the cold, damp sand, I looked back at where I had walked. There were now two sets of footprints in the sand. He was no longer carrying me in His loving arms. We were now walking side by side. As the waves crashed ever so gently against the shore, they echoed my name.

Forgetting the pain and memories of my past, I felt like a kid with sand between my toes, a cool breeze sweeping across my face, and the birds singing in the air. Looking across the endless ocean where the water met the sky reminded me of the beauty of God's creation. Every day God paints a new canvas for us—both magnificent and ever changing. Yet we often take this beautiful gift for granted. We go to art shows and marvel over the many paintings, yet a greater masterpiece surrounds us daily.

Another day passed, and I was still waiting for the doctor to plan my upcoming treatments. Waiting seems to be the most challenging part for me. I'm continuing to learn to trust. Such an easy word to say but not always easy to do. My nights were filled with unending seizures that plagued my body. Like being a prisoner with no way to escape torment and pain. My body shook uncontrollably as I tried to catch my breath in between. My heart filled with such fear as my life flashed before my eyes. I was crying out for God to take this pain from me. I felt abandoned and alone as I did twenty years ago.

CHAPTER 8

Finding Faith

Over twenty years ago, my friendship with Sandi Jo had ended on a rocky road and not the ice-cream type. Some may have thought my behavior rebellion. In truth, I was searching for my own identity, trying to find me. How could I care about someone else when I didn't care about myself or know who I was? I'd overcome an accident that changed my life forever but got lost in the pain that overtook my life.

After graduating from high school and accepting Jesus into my heart, I went through some rugged valleys. Over the years, I discovered that one must go through the valleys to reach the mountaintop.

Sandi Jo tried to mentor and love me as I prepared to leave Plymouth, Indiana, and move to Bowman Hall Dorm at IWU. I loved her with all I was capable of. Although I longed for someone to care for me, I didn't know what love was.

Living with Sandi Jo, I spent hours listening to her sing and prepare for her concerts on her black, baby grand piano in the corner of her living room. The music echoed through the air and ministered to my soul. These memories will always remain embedded in my heart.

Along with the precious times we spent together came struggles. But one struggle we couldn't move beyond ended up taking us down different roads. We encountered a diversion that led us down a big hill on the side of her house into her garden full of weeds that emulated our friendship and lives.

Looking at the many weeds that filled the garden, she explained that the garden was much like our lives. Her tears flowed as she started pulling weeds. The more the tears flowed, the more weeds she pulled.

Sandi looked at me with tear-filled eyes. "Life is much like these weeds," she said. "If the weeds overtake the fruit of the crops, all you have left is weeds. You must take time to pull the weeds before they overtake the garden or your life."

At that moment, I heard everything she was saying, but how in the world did she expect me to pull the weeds out of my life? I couldn't open my body and pull the weeds out. While it made sense, I didn't have an instruction book.

When we finished pulling the weeds, I left the garden feeling abandoned by all who knew and loved me. I was lost spiritually, emotionally, and mentally. I was in a scary place, yet at the same time was in the best place to be as God wrapped His arms around me and taught me what love was. The love that only He can give because "God is love" (1 John 4:8). He became my Rock, my secret refuge, and my hiding place.

Over the next twenty years, Sandi Jo and I saw each other only a couple times. Our struggle built a cliff between us, one we couldn't bridge. As my graduation from IWU approached, I reached out to Sandi. She'd been influential in my going to IWU; I wanted to thank her for guiding me there and share this day with her. We met for coffee—sharing both tears and remembering happier times. The pieces of our lives, however, were scattered like a puzzle. I was no longer the teenage girl she once knew but was a young woman who suffers an invisible illness with no cure.

Although we both desired to put the pieces back together, we struggled to find matching pieces. No matter how hard someone tries to put pieces together, they won't fit if they're from different puzzles. Our puzzles of life were no longer one but separate.

Sandi wanted nothing more than to mend the broken pieces, but she struggled as she watched me suffer. No matter how hard she tried, she could do nothing to fix or to fill in the gaps in the broken and missing pieces of my life. She finally realized she could do nothing more. This became too much for her to bear.

No one can do anything to take away the pain. No one can fix me. Two simple words soften the heavy load I carry—I care. These two words shine God's light brighter in my darkness. In every moment of life, you have an opportunity to minister to those around you. You have an opportunity to be Jesus with skin on.

I don't fear dying, but sometimes I fear living. I don't want people to see this side of me. I do not want them to know that the warrior they see in me is merely a child as described in the song, "Warrior is a Child," by Twila Paris.

Tired and weary from the battle, Donna and I prepared for another twelve-hour trip down the long, winding roads through the mountains of Ohio, Pennsylvania, and into Baltimore.

Late that night, we checked into the hotel next to Johns Hopkins Hospital. I walked over to the window that overlooked the one-hundred-thirty-acre hospital campus in the middle of Baltimore, Maryland. Anxiety consumed me from the inside out, and tears flowed down my cheeks. I only wanted to go back home. Hours passed as the night grew darker and mimicked the pain and despair I felt.

Finally, in the wee hours of the morning, when I dozed off, my body began to convulse and grow limp like a rag doll. The pressure in my head built, my eyes grew dim, and everything became dark from the swelling of my optic nerves.

With little or no sleep, we drove to the infusion center. My veins were tired and weak as the nurses repeatedly poked me to find a vein. Once the needle finally threaded the vein, the meds dripped slowly into my hand and traveled through every vessel in my body, burning like wildfire as it invaded my mind and body, leaving me lifeless.

I tried to fight the medications. I tried to overcome the pain and extreme drowsiness by browsing through my phone, which became consumed with ads. Agitated, I flipped to the next screen to an advertisement for IWU. The ad was for a 100 percent online degree. I was surprised by how far they'd come since I'd been on campus in 1995. Curious about all they had to offer, I requested more information.

Several hours later, the meds had taken over. After ten bags of meds, I struggled to get on the shuttle back to the hotel. Swaying from one side to the next, I felt the world spinning around me, and I was about to lose control. The ten-minute ride seemed like hours, and the noise around me sounded as though it were amplified through a megaphone. Back at the hotel, we had everything we needed before heading to our room, where I crashed on the bed.

I'd dozed off when the phone rang. The admission counselor at IWU said he was calling to finish the application process. Application for what? I didn't know what they were talking about, and thought I was in a dream. Then I realized what I'd done. Instead of requesting information about their online courses, I applied to attend IWU online. After twenty years, I had given up on this chapter of my life because I thought it was over.

Excited about the prospect of continuing my education, I went to my appointment at Johns Hopkins the next morning. I shared this development with my doctor, only for him to take all the joy from me. "Your health challenges will never permit you to complete your academics." She went on to list all the reasons I couldn't do it on my own. But I could see no reason why I couldn't do it with God. What did I have to lose from trying?

With so many questions in my heart and mind, I prayed for God to show me His plan. I'd been accepted at IWU only by the hand of God. He opened a door I thought had been closed forever. He gave me back a piece of my life that had been stolen from me.

A few months later, I began school. As the doctor had warned, I struggled daily to finish my work. Yet, for the first time since my illness, I felt like I was living despite my pain and treatments. I felt like God had given me a purpose. I was no longer merely surviving. I felt like I'd begun living again. The continued trips to Johns Hopkins now included the challenge of completing my homework as we traveled.

On one trip, we arrived at Johns Hopkins Hospital on March 20, 2014, to prepare for my procedure the next day. After the tests, Donna, Arlene, and I went to see the movie *God is Not Dead*. I loved it! At the end of the movie, they said to text everyone you know, *God is Not Dead!* Yet, I couldn't focus on that because the Scripture reference of Mark 5 repeated in my head.

We left the theater and walked down the hall when I realized the pressure was gone. I told Donna and Arlene about the pressure and the verse flooding my mind. I didn't know what Mark 5:34 was or why it kept playing in my head. Arlene took her pocket Bible out of her purse and read, "Daughter, your faith has made you well; go in peace and be healed of your disease" (Mark 5:34). She and Donna shed tears as I stood there in shock.

What did this mean? We stood there a moment as I questioned, "Could this be real? Is it really happening to me?" We left the theater and went to my next appointment at Johns Hopkins to have the fluid drained.

When we entered the exam room, I told the doctor that the pressure behind my eyes and in my head was gone. She examined me and said the swelling of my optic nerve had decreased. She insisted it couldn't be gone because she had seen it a few hours earlier. I explained to her what had happened, and while she was still trying to figure it out, I knew God had drained that fluid for me.

The doctor, not believing in the miracle, insisted on continuing the procedure to check the pressure and drain the fluid. Prepped for the spinal tap, I knew she needed to do this to confirm what I'd been telling her. She explained the pressure was down, and the fluid didn't need to be drained.

The doctor never admitted to the miracle performed by God but did admit that something had happened to change my pressure. God is in control and bigger than any illness or storm in our lives. We must remember that if we don't see an answer now, it doesn't mean no!

Back home the next day, my birthday, I prepared for my knee surgery. Not how I wanted to spend the day, but this was the only time the doctor was available to do it. When I returned to my room after surgery, I was given a sock monkey. I don't know how I named him or where the name came from, but I called him Mooky the Monkey. From then on, Mooky went with me to all my medical treatments and visits.

On one of my visits to Plymouth Hospital, they struggled to get an IV into my hand. After several pokes, the nurse put a cute Band-Aid on my finger and a matching one on Mooky's hand. This was the beginning of a ministry

God prepared me for. Each time I returned to a hospital or doctor's office, the nurse put a bandage on Mooky to represent what I had done. The nurses and I bonded during this time, and Mooky began filling with bandages, IVs, and stitches.

Finishing my associate's degree and getting accepted into my bachelor's degree in communication was a defining moment for me. I reached out to Sandi to share my accomplishments with her. This day was filled with joy and fear as I embarked on a new direction in my life.

As I prepared for graduation, I was in the middle of setting up book tours for a dear author friend and talking with authors and publishers. As an assistant to the author, I had the honor of driving her to the different locations and working with her fans and the bookstore. People came from hours away with the hope of a hug and an autograph from her. She inspired me to continue writing my story and to follow my dream of writing while fulfilling my degree. God had placed me where I needed to be to find the courage to share my story in the pages of this book.

The book tour led us down the rolling hills and breathtaking waters in Wisconsin into Minnesota, where the author met with the publisher near the Mall of America, the largest mall in the United States and Western Hemisphere. The adventure of a lifetime was beckoning me. But the excitement of the Mall of America crashed to the ground when I realized it wasn't everything I'd envisioned it to be.

This mall is a dream for anyone who loves to shop: three floors of stores, a myriad of people strolling hallways longer than streets, and maps larger than some of our small towns. Yet there was nothing cozy or warm about it. The Mall of America is filled with bright, bold colors reflected by bright lights and rambunctious noises. Where else can you shop and visit an amusement park at the same time?

Walking the winding hallways overwhelmed me, and I got lost in the crowd moments after arriving. We reached the food court filled with people eating and watching loved ones and friends riding rides. We decided to ride the Ferris wheel, which lifted us above the world and into the many adventures around us. That's when I spotted the Pepsi Orange Streak Roller Coaster. Can you believe it was calling my name?

Leaving the Ferris wheel, we headed toward the entrance to the roller coaster. Donna was excited and ready for the adventure. I was brave and confident as I walked the steps to the landing and buckled in. The car began to climb the small hill, which seemed like a mountain in front of us. That's when I realized it was much bigger than it appeared. After climbing to the top, but before we dropped from the cliff, I asked Donna, "Have I completely lost my mind?"

I wouldn't say I like roller coasters, and I'm deathly afraid of heights. How in the world did I end up here? After a few screams, I closed my eyes, which magnified the experience intensely. Up the hill and around the curve to drop again. We caught a quick breath before we slowly climbed the final mountain and instantly dropped three stories to our final farewell. Although the ride was only a few minutes, I was exhausted by our Mall of America adventures, or should I say The Pepsi Streak Roller Coaster adventure, in particular.

Now my stomach was twisted and turned inside out. Donna decided she was hungry. We spotted The Hard Rock Cafe, where I met their young, delightful manager named Jessica. After conversing and sharing our adventures, I shared a small bit of my testimony. Tears slowly built in her eyes as she shared how her brother also suffered from a traumatic brain injury. We felt an immediate connection that could only come from an understanding of the illness and the long journey that comes with it.

Although I didn't shop or venture through many of the halls of the Mall of America, God brought me there for that moment both Jessica and I needed. Upon leaving the mall, all I could think about was the time spent with Jessica and how amazing God is to place us where we need to be at the right time. God is never surprised by what lies ahead. He gives us what we need precisely when we need it. "The heart of man plans his way, but the LORD establishes his steps" (Proverbs 16:9).

After arriving home from our trip, we prepared for the day I thought would never happen—my graduation from IWU. We spent days planning a party to share with my friends and family all God has done in my life. Because of my love for horses, I organized a Kentucky Derby-themed party with unique, elegant hats like those worn by women attending the Kentucky Derby. People showed up to my party with hats that represented their personalities, while others searched for hats that reminded them of their past, like Jane, who spent hours online searching for the perfect hat from the '20s. The hat fit Jane's personality perfectly. She and her daughter, Lynn, never missed a moment to celebrate all I had done over the years.

Friends continued to fill the barn as the hats went from elegant to western and some fun and adventures. This was only one of the many memories I cherished with them.

People came from miles away and from different stages of my life: family, including my parents, my brother and his family, my aunt Vera, and Donna, who is like family; friends Debra, Sandi, and Ed, and persons who've been part of my treatment and recovery: Rosie, my first physical therapist and Kathy, my current physical therapist. Even many of my elementary and high school teachers celebrated with me, along with some friends you have yet to meet—Pam and Steve, and Judy and Richard.

My brother Ron DJ'd the party, while my friend Mewsette taught line dancing. Many enjoyed dancing while others played cornhole toss. The tables were filled with people reminiscing about the past and talking about the present, but most of all, showing how proud they were of all I had accomplished.

Kaitlyn from Presley Jane Photograph captured the day—a day I will always cherish. While I was in the distance being pulled from one person to another, Kaitlyn ensured she got pictures of everyone and the moments I spent with them.

The tables were filled with southern fried chicken, salad, chips, cheese, crackers, and veggies, but nothing could compare to the beautiful cupcakes that sat on the wood stumps. They were like lights and a fountain. The cupcakes were decorated with red roses with white pearls to represent the bed of roses which is laid on the winning horse's back. Stephanie from La D'zert spent hours perfecting my cupcakes and even making a mini cake as her special gift to me. They added elegance, with a taste of perfection.

I will never forget that day in the horse barn at Centennial Park, where I spent many hours playing as a child, and now, I was celebrating a day that seemed impossible—my graduation. The doors were lined with friends, elementary teachers, high school teachers, medical staff, my family, Sandi and Ed, and Debra, my angel from my accident.

After graduating, my life went in a new direction as I began writing in my journal. Here I shared my deepest secrets, pain, and fears. The blank pages filled with the untold stories within my heart.

Blank Pages

Over the years, I learned that my journal was my friend.
When I felt I had nowhere to go, my journal was always there.

FINDING FAITH IN THE STORM

> From as long ago as I can remember,
> I would sit daily and write.
> Like having a friend I could share everything with.
> As I grew older, my life became consumed by all around me,
> And the pages in my journal remained blank.
> Until I picked up my pen the day after graduation,
> And the words filled the pages as tears flowed down my cheeks.
> My journal was always my safe place.
> I didn't have to pretend to be OK when I really was not OK.
> My body was failing me, and my smiles were often deceiving.
> The pages were filled with my cries of pain and fear.
> I often find myself trying to be the courageous and strong girl everyone thinks I am.
> But inside, I feel like falling apart and crying.
> Those are the times I'm reminded that God is there with me.

Continuing my trips to Johns Hopkins Hospital became more than I could bear. Some things are easier to remember, and some things you can't forget. Yet returning to see Dr. Paula after a year of trips to Johns Hopkins is a moment I'll always remember as if it happened yesterday.

Here, starting on the next page, is my paper I wrote to share because it's a big part of my story.

Who's in the Next Stall?

Life is full of memories. Sometimes we recall these memories and smile while other times we may chuckle. Looking back at one of my most embarrassing moments brings joy to my heart.

I live with chronic migraines, which force me to go to the doctor on a regular basis. My migraines had reached a point where I was no longer living my life; they were living it for me. I would wake up with a blinding pain—inside and out. My neurologist had tried everything she knew to do and even more. Eventually, realizing she couldn't do it alone, Dr. Paula sent me to Johns Hopkins Hospital in Baltimore, Maryland, the number one rated hospital in neurology. Although the hospital was excellent, the care was less personable.

In early dawn, I would arrive for a treatment or procedure and stand in line, waiting among many other patients from all over the world. We were recognized by numbers instead of the names printed next to them. Called one by one like an assembly line, we'd move down the row, completing all the necessary paperwork. After completing the paperwork, I was told to sit and wait in a room filled with unfamiliar faces in an unfamiliar city. I saw the faces of many nations filled with pain and despair, while I hid in a corner.

I traveled back and forth to a place where I felt alone and lost. After several months had passed, the time came to see my neurologist, Dr. Paula.

Her staff greeted me with a smile and my name, "Hello, Pebbles."

I was no longer just a number. I was somebody. I found peace within myself. This was where I belonged. A myriad of emotions built inside me as I waited to see Dr. Paula. My head filled with chaos as the questions rapidly filled my mind.

What if she's not happy with their ideas?

What if she is not happy with my progress?

And the worst: *What if she sends me back to Johns Hopkins Hospital?*

I heard papers rustle outside the door, then Paula turned the knob and walked in. Here was the moment I'd been anticipating with joy and fear. Dr. Paula beamed a warm smile that eased all my fears. She understood me. She cared. She saw me as more than a number but as a person for whom she wanted to do all she could.

She took the time to review all the treatment options and personalize them for me, bringing me hope again.

Donna and I went down a long hall to the bathroom. I went into one stall while Donna entered the other one (or I should say I thought she went into the other one). Believing we were the only two in the bathroom, I shared the hope I felt in my heart.

I reviewed my appointment details. "It was so nice walking into Dr. Paula's office where the staff recognize me as a person they cared about. Dr. Paula wants to do all she can to help me live the best life I can despite my illness. She even complimented me on my hair and was glad to see me."

After about five minutes of me going on about how much I love Paula as my neurologist, I stepped out of the stall. There stood Donna, pointing to the stall next to me. I hadn't been talking to her at all!

I almost fell to the floor in embarrassment when I realized it was not Donna in the next stall but Dr.

Paula! I couldn't wash my hands fast enough. *What did she think of me now?*

During the silence that penetrated the air, I rushed to open the door to the hall that now seemed even longer than before. Stopping for a moment, I caught a glimpse of Paula passing by. With a quick exchange of smiles, I continued out the door, embarrassed for sharing praise for a doctor I respect and trust in every way.

It's easy to lose faith in battling the obstacles before me. I began questioning God's plan for my life and where He is or if He cares. Yet He is faithful to show me how He works in and through my circumstances, providing the people and doctors I need along the way.

CHAPTER 9

OVERCOMING THE ODDS

My body was tired and weak as I approached my final year of classes for my bachelor's degree in communications. The lessons became more difficult as my health became more challenging. I spent most of the year in the hospital facing multiple surgeries. While preparing for a major surgery and finishing my last class, Donna and I headed to Virginia Beach with Ron. This place had become our Christmas getaway.

We spent time listening to the ocean as I filled many pages of my final capstone project on "Connected, but Alone." The project was about social media and how it has overtaken the world. The title represented how I felt with my family and friends. Many would call and ask how I was doing,

"I'm OK," I'd respond, and then they'd hang up and continue their day.

The truth is, I am never really OK. I'm living with an illness that has invaded my body and holds me prisoner to daily pain.

I treasured the time spent on the beach because it renewed my mind and spirit. The beach is my sacred place away from all the doctors and hospitals. It's a place where I can escape the reality of my illness.

At the beach, we rode bikes, flew kites, walked in the sand, played games, and went to dinner with Arlene and Dan.

For one week, I was able to forget all I was going through and live again, cherishing moments with my brother. With the balcony door opened, we listened to the waves lapping while the smell of the ocean scented the air. We watched the beautiful sunrise over the surfers lined up to catch the morning waves.

Navy jets flew over with loud thunder reminiscent of the moments spent there with my brother, Tim, who passed away over fifteen years ago. I felt his presence there with us as we visited the navy memorials and even the lighthouse on the naval base. Those who leave us are never entirely gone. We hold them in our hearts forever.

This trip was different than others as Ron prepared to run in the Yuengling Shamrock Marathon. He dressed in fluorescent green on a cold, brisk Virginia day and was ready to run among over twenty thousand runners. People of all ages and different skill levels ran through the streets of Virginia Beach to the three-mile boardwalk at the finish line.

I was amazed to see people with disabilities, children, parents, and families run together. I was inspired to see my brother pass by with a smile on his face. Maybe one day, I'll be among the many who pass under the finish banner. Maybe one day, I'll have the courage and strength to complete my first marathon. I learned it's not about winning but about achieving your dream.

The marathon complete, the streets emptied as we prepared to go home the next day—a day I always dreaded. The week passed by quickly, and we loaded everything into the car and bid farewell to the hotel manager, Sarah, who continues to be a blessing to me.

The cold car warmed with laughter and music as we traveled back down the long, twisting roads of Virginia, West Virginia, and Ohio. Long talks carried us through the mountains and around the curves, much like the memories of our childhood. We each faced many mountains and winding roads in our lives. We spent the twelve-hour drive home talking about our childhood and sharing what was happening in the world and how it became what it is today, sharing our faith, struggles, and victories. We said our goodbyes to Dan and Arlene, not knowing this would be the last time Ron would see Dan before Dan's passing a few years later. I will always cherish the precious memories of our time together.

We got home that day in time to be admitted into the hospital for another major surgery two weeks before graduation. This time, the surgeon cut me from hip to hip and put one drain tube on one side and another on the other. I called them Thing One and Thing Two. With Mooky at my side, the nurses emulated all I had done on him. They replicated drain tubes and staples that looked like the railroad track that crossed my lower abdomen, reminiscent of the hernia surgery years before. The staples pulled and irritated while the drain tubes constantly got in the way.

The doctor made an appointment with me the day before graduation to take out my staples. Although he thought it was still a bit early to remove them, he did so with the understanding that I'd come back on Monday to ensure everything was okay and to see if they'd have to be put back in. I had such a good feeling getting everything removed. However, the pain was still intense while I prepared to be the graduation speaker the following day.

Not only was I graduating with honors, but the marketing department of IWU also invited me to film a commercial for their Shine Brighter Campaign, and the faculty chose me as the graduation speaker. This honor provided an opportunity for me to share my ministry with The Mooky Project. Mooky is the sock monkey Donna got for me at one of my surgeries. Mooky plays a huge role in my treatment process. IWU got Mooky a cap and gown to wear in our photo session before graduation.

After the photo shoot, I stood at the beginning of the procession line at the entrance to the chapel, reminiscent of my senior year of high school when this moment was taken from me. Lost in the memory, "Pomp and Circumstance" began to play as the tears flooded my eyes. I did it! I overcame the odds of what the doctor said I could never do.

Despite spending over two hundred days in the hospital bed working on homework during surgeries and treatments, I was graduating!

As I walked proudly down the aisle to the music, out of the corner of my eye, I saw my brother Ron and Donna clapping.

This was more than I could've ever imagined. As I walked from my seat to the stage to speak, I heard my name from the top of the balcony. Donna and my brother Ron were sitting near the stage, so I knew it wasn't one of them.

The seats in the chapel were filled, and anxiety built up in me as I painfully walked up the steps to the left side of the stage.

What if I mess up?

What if everyone gets bored with my speech?

As they announced my name, I slowly walked toward the lectern and prayed, *God, I give this to you. It's not about me but about you living in me.*

As I got to the lectern and looked around the room, my words flowed through me by the power of the Holy Spirit.

FINDING FAITH IN THE STORM

My Graduation Speech 2018

I am not standing here because of my own accomplishments; I am standing here to represent each of you and the battles we fought to get here today. A day filled with laughter, joy, and tears as we reach a milestone in our lives. What can we, as a diverse class, offer to those around us? Faith, hope, and love!

Without hope, I would not be here today!

I am battling an illness that people can't see with their eyes—pseudotumor cerebri and chronic daily migraines. These have invaded my body, trying to hold me captive to the pain I suffer daily. I've learned that it's not about being strong but about being weak so Jesus can be strong in me.

My name is Pebbles Wireman. I am forty-four years old. Growing up, I struggled to know what love was. The first time I heard the song "Jesus Loves Me," I did not know who Jesus was and why He would love me. My life was in shambles, and everything seemed hopeless until March 13, 1992, when Jesus shined his light into my darkness. As I wept, He took me into His arms and held me, wiping the tears from my eyes. That was the first moment I knew what love is. God's love! A love that is beyond anything we could ever imagine.

After graduating in 1992, I did not know where God was leading me. Attending IWU here on campus and becoming hall president was the beginning of many changes. Yet the biggest change happened when a car T-boned me that summer, and all my dreams were crushed into the ground. I thought this chapter of my life was over.

As my health continues to decline, much of my life is spent in hospitals, including Johns Hopkins Hospital, where I was when I saw an advertisement for IWU. I clicked on it, knowing I could never go back to school with my health. Yet before I knew it, God began to write a new chapter in my life, one that includes IWU. "Jesus looked at them and said, 'With man, this is impossible, but with God, all things are possible'" (Matthew 19:26 NIV). He is a God of hope.

But what is hope without faith?

I continue to walk by faith as I enter Wesley Seminary for a Master of Arts in Ministry and Worship Arts. I will apply my God-given gifts of compassion, love, and forgiveness to those around me, leading others through the valleys and over the trenches into the arms of Jesus Christ.

The education I have received from Indiana Wesleyan has prepared me for a ministry to children in the hospital. The Mooky Project began when I received a sock monkey in the hospital. He went everywhere with me, getting band-aids, IVs, stitches, and an ID bracelet M-O-O-K-Y—Mooky. I do not know where the name came from, but it means fun, adventurous, and enduring. What better name for him? IWU has challenged me to be a world changer, reaching out to kids in faith and love while making a difference in their treatment process.

Love brings faith and hope!

Whether it is the love of your family, friends, or instructors, each of us holds different people close to our hearts as we look back at the countless hours of studying. And let's not forget God! How many of you called out to God at 11:58 p.m. the night before a paper was due at midnight, expecting a miracle? I know I have. Whether you reached the deadline or not, God was there.

Although all my instructors helped me achieve the impossible, there are three here today who believed in me, loved me, and prayed with me every step of the way. I want to especially thank Professors CT, Dr. Penny McCann-Washer, and Dr. Henry Smith. You gave me hope when things seemed hopeless and believed in me when I did not believe in myself. Thank you for pushing me beyond what I thought I could achieve.

I also want to thank my family, friends, and medical teams who believed in me. Yet there is one person who has fought the battles with me. My caregiver and friend, Donna Strite, loved me through the countless hours of schoolwork and the many tears of completing it.

A well-known saying goes, "Stop and Smell the Roses." But I would like to change that to "Stop and Share God's Love." We are called together as a unity of believers to be world changers. Now, let's all stand together in victory as we go out and change the world!

As I shared my story, there were moments of laughter, cheers, and even tears from the audience. I knew then God had used me to touch the lives of many of the graduates. I left the stage and sat in the front row as I awaited the moment when I would receive my diploma. I'd worked hard over the past few years while getting treatments and surgeries, and I felt proud of my accomplishments.

I walked across the stage to accept my diploma and shook President Wright's hand. Tears welled in my eyes as I heard my name shouted from the balcony again. I tried to figure out who it could be, to no avail.

The graduation ceremony ended, and we walked in a procession out the door and ran into many who told me how my speech touched their hearts. This was a moment etched in my heart forever. I continued to walk past the crowd toward the student center when I was surprised to see my fourth-grade teacher, Mr. Scarberry, and his wife, Cheryl, standing there.

Wow! I can never tell you how much it meant that they would drive almost two hours for my graduation. What a moment of surprise as I solved the mystery of who was yelling from the balcony. We went to lunch together and reminisced about my years at West Elementary with Mrs. Espich, Mrs. Newburg, and Mrs. Tyree, who all significantly influenced my educational journey, enabling me to become who I am today.

I got home late that evening. Exhausted, I got everything together and headed to the horse barn where my graduation party would be held the next day. I was alone at the barn, decorating throughout the night, and my pain overtook me. But then people started showing up to help decorate and bring the supplies I needed—Ron, Judy and Richard, and Sandi and Ed.

We finished barely an hour before my graduation hoedown. I hurried home to get a shower and get dressed, but I was so tired I wanted to crawl under the blankets. No time to stop for even a moment before heading back with Donna.

People were gathered by the door when I returned. I greeted them with smiles and hugs. The day was filled with family and friends sharing laughter and tears.

FINDING FAITH IN THE STORM

Many took part in the activities throughout the day. Line dancing led by Mewsette with music played by my brother Ron. Debra's grandson, Jaxson, sang a song while others played corn hole toss and Cracker Barrel checkers. The smell of fried chicken cascaded through the barn, with La D'zert Cupcakes cascading down like a waterfall.

Mookys were hidden throughout the barn, reminding me why I want to continue with my education—to make The Mooky Project all it can be. We all celebrated something we never thought possible. We celebrated God bringing me through another hurdle in life with honors.

People left as evening approached. Many stayed into the night to help clean up. Now, the time came to say goodbye, go home, and prepare for the film crew to arrive early the next morning to film the Shine Brighter Campaign commercial for IWU.

I didn't sleep much that night. I was nervous about filming the commercial the next day and exhausted from all the graduation activities. The pain began to overtake my very being. I was still trying to recover from my surgery, and all the activities began to take a toll on me. I woke at six a.m. with a migraine. I struggled to get myself together, praying for God to get me through one more day.

My smile disguised the pain and tears building up inside, but I trusted God.

Through every storm I face, I keep asking myself, "Do I trust you, Lord?" Even though I may not know what the next step will be, I know God is guiding my steps along the way. He already knows what my journey is and is preparing me along the way.

"Yes, I trust you, Lord."

One by one, vehicles arrived in front of our house. One for hair and makeup; one for snacks; one for camera equipment; and one for the rest of the film crew. I had no idea what was to come. What had I agreed to?

The film crew came to the door and explained the filming process. They had a makeup and hair person for me and were prepared for anything I might need during the day. What I thought would be an hour or two ended up being ten hours of filming.

After my hair and makeup were done, we headed to the park. We walked across the bridge to the walking trail behind the big hill to a beautiful landscape where a major part of the filming was done. The squirrels were hustling up the trees as the leaves rustled that spring morning.

I had no idea what it took to film a five-minute commercial. I quickly learned it involves lots of repetition. Time after time, I repeated the words and actions, doing my best to smile through the pain. After hours of walking down the lane and sharing my story as Donna and Debra sat close by, we headed to our house where we would have lunch and film the Mooky part of the commercial.

One film crew went to get us lunch while another helped pick out a new outfit for me.

"Ready to go to the second part of the filming?" the crew asked.

Hardly.

But we quickly ate, finished my hair and makeup, and prepared to film again. This part included Donna, Debra, and Pam, who were all part of The Mooky Project.

Pam and Debra showed up at our door carrying boxes. They came into the house, and we excitedly opened the boxes to reveal our first Mookys. We loaded the Mookys into the car and then we all piled into cars and started the procession to Thorin's house, a boy who would receive our first Mooky. He has been through much but continues to battle with his parents and family at his side.

We arrived and talked to his mom before beginning the filming process. Hair and makeup were done again, and we were ready to deliver Mooky.

Donna, Debra, and I walked up to the door and entered the kitchen, where Thorin sat in his chair. I sat next to him as I handed him Mooky. Thorin cuddled right up to Mooky and smiled from ear to ear. Thorin stole my heart as he loved Mooky. I pray that every Mooky brings a smile to children's faces. I pray it helps them to have a buddy at their side as they go through their treatment process. Mooky helped me over the years and has been at my side through it all.

We ended the visit with lots of hugs and the final filming before heading home, where I could finally lay down and rest. My energy was gone, but my heart was full. The commercial turned out to be more than I could've ever imagined. They did a fantastic job of sharing my story and Mooky's too. They did a great job conveying how IWU helped me achieve the impossible as I continue to follow God's leading.

CHAPTER 10

THE MOOKY PROJECT

With the completion of my Bachelor of Science Degree in Communications in April 2018, I was ready for a new experience. Despite repeated doctor visits, hospitalizations, and six major surgeries, I completed my undergraduate courses. While preparing for the next part of my educational journey, I worked toward a ministry to bring comfort and joy to children in the hospital—The Mooky Project.

The Mooky Project became my heart's passion to help bring joy and hope to children in the hospital, despite their pain. Starting a ministry in the hospital presented many challenges due to the guidelines put in place by the hospital to protect the children. Yet I didn't let that discourage me from following God's leading and call on my life.

Wesley Seminary became one step toward overcoming these challenges. Getting a degree in ministry and becoming ordained allows me to visit the children when I give them a treatment buddy—Mooky. It's not about the sock monkey but sharing God's love and compassion during their pain and suffering. A simple act of kindness makes such a difference when you feel alone and scared.

My first class at Wesley Seminary was led by the president of the seminary, Dr. Colleen Derr. During this class, we prepared our mission statement for our ministry. This required assessing the challenges and embracing the sacred pilgrimage God prepared for us. Dr. Derr challenged me to think bigger. She taught me we are only limited by our own goals and dreams.

I faced many challenges as I began The Mooky Project. However, this class helped me to see beyond the obstacles and how to overcome them effectively. Children from many cultures, religions, backgrounds, and disabilities are in the hospital. Despite their different backgrounds, they have similar personality traits, wants, and desires.

Because I've spent so much time in the hospital, I can relate to the children at a different level than people who've never experienced what they have. I continue to seek God's guidance and direction as I minister to these kids and share God's love. Children in the hospital look at life differently than most kids and appreciate simple things like crafts, being outside, and spending time with family and friends. By analyzing myself, the room, and the children, I've developed ways to overcome the challenges by embracing the blessings within my ministry with The Mooky Project

We are all great in the eyes of God. "For we are his workmanship, created in Christ Jesus for good works, which God prepared beforehand, that we should walk in them" (Ephesians 2:10). I continue to seek growth physically, mentally, spiritually, and relationally as I mature in Christ. As I analyze myself, I look at where I've been, where I am now, and where I want to be.

Despite these many things, I cannot change in ministering to the children, I've learned by changing the environment around the patients, I can develop a bright and happy atmosphere. Although I cannot change the children's pain, I can help change how they feel emotionally and spiritually. Each child I work with comes from a different background and spiritual development. Along with their zest for life, they dislike the things they are unable to do and want to be able to run and play like other kids their age. Mooky is there to bring joy and comfort during their pain and suffering.

The Mooky Project is a ministry formed to help children in the hospital through their treatment process. Working with children from various hospitals creates a diverse group of children from different lifestyles and backgrounds. Therefore, each child is at a different point in their faith. Some come to the hospital without knowing God, while others have spent their entire lives in church and Sunday school. While each of them has a different level of knowledge, they're hungry to learn about God and His love for them. Interestingly, sometimes I go into a patient's room ready to build their faith, yet I leave with my faith strengthened.

These children range from newborn to sixteen, which is a wide range of levels of comprehension and understanding. Still, they all carry a love and passion in their heart I've never seen before. They've learned something some people may never know—how precious life is. Battling an illness changes your perspective and view on life, which makes children love with all their hearts.

Although much of their life is spent in the hospital battling their illness, they don't allow it to hinder their hopes and dreams, though some of them will never live to see their goals fulfilled. Paul's prayer for the Ephesians points to a paradox: faith formation is not complete in this life, but even so, it is goal oriented. Paul describes the goal this way: "That you may be filled to the measure of all the fullness of God" (Eph. 3:19 NIV). Children don't allow challenges to defeat them. Their lives aren't about what they can't do but what they can do despite their health. Their faith and courage often make them stronger because they aren't limited by the goals and limits set upon them by others.

With a goal of providing twenty Mookys a year to children in the hospital, I received a call from Riley's Children's Hospital while I was in another hospital recovering from major surgery. They asked if I could provide Mookys to the children in their hospital for Christmas. I don't know if the pain medicine had a hold of me or what, but I said yes.

Immediately, I called my team. Donna and Debra quickly said OK. But Pam knew for sure my pain meds had overpowered my mind when I agreed to find sponsors for over three-hundred children in less than two weeks. All three of them knew me well enough to know I never let anything stop me or hold me back, so they decided to agree now and ask questions later.

After my meds wore off, I began to question myself. How was I going to raise over $6000 in two weeks? I knew it was impossible for me to do on my own, but "With God, all things are possible" (Matthew 19:26).

Through faith, we got over three-hundred sponsors in two weeks, and my brother Ron, Donna, Pam, and I were tagging three hundred fifty Mookys to prepare for delivery on Christmas Eve. We loaded the car so full Donna could barely peek through the hundreds of Mookys surrounding her. Ann met us at the door and unloaded them into crates to be taken in and safety checked in time for Christmas morning. After spending time with Ann and taking pictures, we headed up to see a special girl, Ivy, to whom I delivered a Mooky with a hug.

Ivy continues to hold a special place in my heart as I follow her courageous journey. She has overcome many health battles and has gone on to graduate and follow her dreams. The Mooky kids become the kids I never had. They become a special part of my life and always leave an imprint on my heart as I follow their journeys.

The Mooky Project continues to grow. I've done many interviews along the way, including one with Fox News at Riley's Children's Hospital, which the president of Wesley Seminary was part of. She spoke about how I said I wanted to do twenty Mookys a year and told me to think bigger. I never imagined three years later I'd have delivered almost three thousand Mookys to children in the hospital. Seeing God at work is an incredible experience. I was closing doors and opening new ones and turning my tests into testimonies, with my continued prayer for God to use me with or without my illness.

CHAPTER 11

From Korea to the USA

Throughout the years, Donna has been a consistent friend and caregiver. Now in her eighties, it has become more difficult for her to do everything she's done before. Therefore, a pastor friend, Dr. V., who was going through a difficult time in life, moved in to help take care of me. We spent two years traveling around the world together and going on multiple cruises to places I had never been and always dreamed of going. During the two years of traveling, I expressed my dream of owning a teacup poodle. Dr. V., who I affectionately call Mama V, reached out to Foufou Puppies on my behalf. She shared my story with them in this letter:

> My name is Dr. V, and I retired last year as a pastor/principal to care for my spiritual daughter, Pebbles Wireman, after she was given six months to live. I am making a special request for one of Foufou's teacup puppies, especially a poodle, for my spiritual daughter's birthday on November 26.
>
> Let me share her story. My spiritual daughter Pebbles Wireman was in a car accident the summer before her senior year. The accident caused a traumatic brain injury and, over the years, has developed into pseudotumor cerebri and chronic daily migraines that leave lesions on her brain.

In the last three years, her medical needs have progressed to the point that her neurologist sends her to Johns Hopkins Hospital in Baltimore, Maryland, for treatment. They are rated number one in neurology.

She refuses to let her health define who she is. She continues to battle through the storms, even doing online schooling when many doctors thought it was impossible for her. She graduated from Indiana Wesleyan University on April 30, 2018, completing many of her assignments from a hospital bed as she fought through the pain and tears to complete them. Not giving up, she has continued to learn online through e-schooling.

She has continued to keep her faith through all of this. She has faith and perseverance!

While she has spent most of the past year in the hospital, her focus is never on herself. Pebbles used her struggles to help kids in the hospital by creating The Mooky Project. The Mooky Project provides treatment buddies to kids in the hospital.

She continues to pursue her dream of getting a doctorate, which her doctors did not know she would ever be able to accomplish with her brain injury. Graduating at the top of her class in 2018 with her bachelor's degree in communications and human services, she not only became the graduation speaker but is also in the school's commercial.

She is currently working on her master's degree online. This past year, she has had multiple surgeries while completing her degree while she continues to use her illness to help encourage others. This past year has been especially challenging with the pandemic and continuing to battle her health despite the extra challenges.

I want to know that Pebbles will always have someone there for her when I am gone. I want her to have a fur baby to hold on to and love when there is no one else to turn to.

Providing over two thousand kids with treatment buddies this past year, she continues to touch the lives of many children in the hospital.

Pebbles is facing a couple major surgeries in the months ahead while continuing her education. She wakes up each morning wondering if she can ever do all she has ever dreamed of, never giving up. Your organization is known for its giving and caring spirit. A service dog would be a blessing to her. Pebbles has had a dream of having a teacup pup. Would you help us celebrate her birthday by making her dream of owning a fur baby like yours come true?

Can you please help to make her dream possible?

Looking forward to hearing from you.

Many Blessings,
Dr. V
Spiritual-mom caregiver

The next morning, Mama V received an email reply from the owner, Sammy. He said my story touched him and his wife so much, they wanted to give me a puppy. After reading Sammy's email, Mama V asked Sammy if he could call and tell me.

He called me moments later as we sat by the pool in Florida. I answered the phone, and Sammy shared about the letter he received and how he wanted to gift a teacup poodle to me, and I could pick any one I wanted. I cried tears of joy as I looked at the puppies on his website. That's when I saw Belle. She stole my heart and became mine. I named her Princess Belle. I couldn't believe she was really mine.

At once, we left to shop for all the necessities on the Foufou Puppies website and found many other things. Going from store to store, her wardrobe became bigger than mine, with more toys than most kids. Princess Belle was not just any puppy. She was now my baby girl.

Later that evening, I got my first video chat with my baby girl. She was a little fluff ball full of energy that loved to play and gave many kisses to the phone. She brought me so much joy; I wanted to take her in my arms and hold her. But I knew it would be several weeks before that day would come because of the restrictions on traveling with the COVID-19 pandemic.

As I patiently, or rather impatiently waited, Sammy at Foufou Puppies ensured I got regular video calls from Princess until we were united at Chicago O'Hare Airport on Dec 14, 2021. Although Sammy couldn't get the travel approved in time for my birthday, Princess arrived in time for Christmas—a perfect gift under my tree. From Korea to Plymouth, Indiana, a puppy found her way home. A Christmas wish granted by Foufou Puppies brought joy and love amid ongoing pain and suffering.

On a cold and snowy early morning, as we prepared to go to O'Hare to pick up Princess Belle, the hours passed slowly as Sammy updated me regularly on her travel. Princess and I had our last video chat before she boarded the plane with a blanket in a dog carrier. I watched her play and felt her love in my heart as Princess licked the phone. She knew she was mine, and I couldn't wait until I could hold her in my arms for the first time.

I couldn't sleep that night, knowing she was all alone on the airplane for over fourteen hours. She was just a baby. Only four months old. Fear rose up inside as I imagined the worst. And tears began to build as I realized the best. I would soon be holding my four-month-old baby girl. Unable to travel with the puppy due to the pandemic, Sammy gave us updates as soon as he received them.

With a photographer following behind, we loaded the car with a warm outfit for Princess, a blanket, food, and a Mooky of her own. The excitement continued to build as we traveled over two hours to pick up my baby girl over snow-filled roads lined with ice-filled trees that glistened in the sun. I was lost in my emotions and feelings. I don't remember much of the drive. My thoughts held me captive until the moment I would meet Princess Belle.

The parking lot was full of people leaving and coming and hustling across the street in the frigid weather. We finally found a parking place near the door. We entered only to find out we had to go next door. There she lay quietly, cuddled up on her blue-plaid blanket in a little ball, peacefully sleeping in her tan carrying case on the floor behind the desk next to the other fur babies.

Although I could see her golden hair through the tiny holes in the case, I couldn't hold her. Time drifted by slowly as we waited for customs to release her. Finally, I heard my name called. Teary-eyed, I was only moments away from holding my baby girl. Anxiously, I walked to the counter and signed all the necessary papers.

They lifted her case onto the counter. She was awake and peeked through a tiny hole in the rigid plastic case, licking my hand as I cut the straps that locked the door. I couldn't get the door open fast enough. Tears of joy flooded my shirt as she jumped into my arms, showering me with love and kisses. Immediately, she cuddled up close to my chest in a tiny ball as we walked to the other side of the building, where I dressed her in a warm snowman sweater and tiny red bows. She was perfect! She was more than I could've imagined.

In a quiet, secluded corner of the tall, white building, we video-called Sammy and thanked him for the gift of love. No words can share what I felt in my heart on that day. No words could express my gratitude for the gift he'd given me or to describe the love I felt for this precious fur baby I now call mine.

We bundled her up in a soft, plush, Mooky blanket, fed her, and prepared her for her trip home. She intently watched out the passenger side window as we traveled the miles down the highway. She didn't want to miss anything.

Near home, we stopped at the house of a friend who is a vet. I wanted to make sure Princess was OK from the long travel. Princess was happy and rambunctious as Dr. Richard took her in his arms and looked her over. With a clean bill of health, she cuddled up in Judy's arms and began kissing her. She knew she was in a place where she was loved. After a short visit, we headed home to meet her GG, Donna.

Donna opened the door with a smile from ear to ear as she took Princess Belle into her arms. "She's perfect!" Donna said as she gently held her close to her face and whispered gently in her ear, "What a sweetie you are."

Mama V and I were exhausted after the long day of travel. But not Princess, who was just waking up. The thirteen-hour time difference from Korea to the United States played a huge role in Princess Belle's adjustment. She loved her new home. She ran and played into the wee hours of the next morning when it was time to get up, and then she was ready to cuddle and sleep. It was much like a human baby who has their days and nights mixed up.

She tilted her head from side to side as I spoke to her as if she didn't understand a word I was saying. Then it dawned on me she spent the first four months of her life in Korea and didn't know English. I began translating words to Korean on my phone. As I struggled to translate the words, Donna and Mama V were filled with laughter. Eventually, getting the words close enough for Princess to understand was a challenge and another obstacle to overcome. Teaching my girl a second language was not something I'd planned for.

FINDING FAITH IN THE STORM

She quickly learned the most essential words and is now fluent in English.

Princess Belle was trained to be my service dog. She goes everywhere with me and helps bring joy to the children in the hospital through The Mooky Project. Shortly after receiving Princess on that cold, December day, we left to go to Florida to spend a month at a resort with Mama V. Princess Belle enjoyed traveling in the car and slept much of the trip.

Arriving late at the condo, we had to unpack the car, which was half filled with Princess's stuff. We took her for walks on the beach, to lighthouses, to Downtown Disney, and relaxed at the pool. Carrying her in a backpack, she was often mistaken for a stuffed animal. The month passed quickly, and we decided to stay a couple more weeks, bringing joy and tears and ending in heartbreak.

CHAPTER 12

THE LAST GOODNIGHT

I never imagined when we went to bed, that night would be the last goodnight. Princes Belle woke me early that Valentine's Day morning and I found my last valentine from Mama V.

> Good morning, my precious Valentine.
> A gift of training and grooming of Belle I give to you.
> Feeding and even cleaning up her poo.
> You have trained her so well on what to do,
> She responded to me as if I were you.
> I am amazed at what you do with her every day.
> I thank and praise God for you in every way.
> So, no cards, flowers, or candy do I have to give,
> But I give of myself that is how God wants us to live.
> So, from my heart to yours, I just want to say
> I love you, and happy Valentine's Day!
> Always & Forever,
> Mama V

After reading the valentine, we prepared to spend the day in the sun. But the sun turned to darkness when Mama V had a chronic obstructive pulmonary disease (COPD) attack. In a moment's response, I caught her in my arms, taking both of us to the ground. I began CPR while waiting for 911 to answer.

1-2-3 breathe 1-2-3 breathe.

"Hello, 911."

"She fell to the ground and isn't responding," I quickly replied. "Her eyes were fixated, and no air was going in!"

They asked for the address and said, "Continue compressions."

1-2-3 breathe 1-2-3 breathe.

Within minutes, the timeshare was filled with EMTs. They threw so many questions me as I watched them intubate her and wrap a machine around her chest to continue machine compressions as they put an IV in her foot. They continued putting meds in the IV with no response.

As they lifted her lifeless body onto the gurney, I gathered my purse and her ID, preparing to follow the ambulance. Princess Belle didn't want to leave her side, nor did I.

I handed Princess Belle to Donna and headed to the elevator. I waited forever for the elevator to reach the sixteenth floor. Watching as they loaded her in the back of the ambulance all seemed like a dream.

I followed the ambulance, but I don't remember the drive or how I got there. When I arrived at the hospital in Celebration, I thought Mama V would be awake and sitting up in bed waiting for me.

Upon entering the ER, I was taken to the room where her body lay limp. They continued to work on her with no response. The room was filled with nurses, doctors, and other medical staff. After nearly an hour passed, the doctor looked toward me in the dark corner and sadly spoke those three letters that changed my life forever.

"DOA."

I knew that meant dead on arrival.

As fast as the room filled with medical staff upon her

entrance, it now emptied. Who would've ever known how much three little letters could change one's life?

I now stood alone in this cold, white room. Only hours earlier, Mama V had been full of life; now she lay lifeless beside me. Tears flowed uncontrollably as I laid my head on her chest. The beating of her heart had stopped, and her breathing was gone. Was this real? How can this be real? I kept thinking I was in a dream and would wake up soon. The reality was that I never woke from that dream. I'm still living it today.

I don't remember the drive back to the resort. Pulling up to the front of the building where the ambulance had parked, I walked toward the elevator they'd taken Mama V down earlier.

My legs felt like marshmallows walking to the door of the suite. With tear-filled eyes, Donna stood there holding Princess Belle. She knew from the look on my face that Mama V was gone. I didn't have to speak a word.

Princess Belle knew something was wrong as she clung to me.

I didn't want to go and leave her behind, but I didn't want to stay without her. I hurriedly packed up the room as the tears continued to flow. We worked around the evidence of her passing left on the floor where they intubated her and started an IV. Trash now filled the space where she once lay.

Late that afternoon when I finished packing everything into the car, I prepared for the long drive home. Knowing I would never be back to the place that became a home away from home and knowing I would never see her again, my heart broke. Princess Belle cuddled up to my chest, licking the tears from my face.

I stopped by the registration desk and left the key, then we drove into the sunset. I felt such an emptiness as I made many phone calls. Mama V's family and friends shared my shock and disbelief.

Suzi had visited us at the resort weeks earlier. Donna's brother, Jeff, spent a week with us, going to Downtown Disney and the lighthouse. None of us would've imagined this would be how it would end.

When I messaged Sammy at Foufou Puppies, he shared Mama V's letter written a couple months earlier. "I want to know that Pebbles will always have someone there for her when I am gone. I want her to have a fur baby to hold on to and love when there is no one else to turn to." Princess Belle was there for me as I held Mama V in my arms the last time and she took her last breath, and she has been there with me every moment since.

Princess Belle was a gift of love that helped bridge the pain that left me paralyzed. I often wonder what Mama V knew when she wrote that letter to Sammy at Foufou Puppies. Did she know God was calling her home? Did she know that it would be that soon? Questions echoed in my mind. Tears flooded my eyes, and pain overtook my heart.

Although we feel the pain of an ending in our lives, Mama V began her eternal life with her heavenly Father. I know she was celebrating that day with those she loved who'd gone before her. Ironically, her celebration began at Celebration Health hospital on Valentine's Day—a day of love. If you knew Mama V, you'd know how appropriate that was.

Rain fell as we left Florida. The tears flowed endlessly down my cheeks, emulating the rain flooding the streets. The farther north we went, the colder it got. The rain turned to ice. Headlights glistened in the ice as it turned darker. Though it was nearly impossible to drive, I couldn't stop. Friends stayed on the phone with me, helping guide me back home amid the cold, dark storm that flooded the streets and my heart.

FINDING FAITH IN THE STORM

The night grew darker as my heart ached harder. My thoughts overtook me as I was lost reliving the moment Mama V fell to the ground. I wished I could've done more, wished I could've saved her. I wanted her here next to me now. I wanted one more goodnight.

We drove through the night. When we finally arrived in our driveway, I was exhausted. The rain and ice had turned to snow and filled the streets and our driveway. Knowing we'd soon be home with a car filled with all we'd taken, and all Mama V left behind, a dear friend, Rachael, and her precious children had shoveled our drive and made snow angels in the front yard before we arrived. They greeted us with open arms and love as we made our way into the house, where packages filled the living room floor.

Mama V had ordered gifts and had them delivered while we were gone. They included a pillow that lay atop the table that said: *Princess Belle's House—Pebbles, Donna, and Dr. V Live Here Too.* As I read those words, my heart crumbled. They were no longer true. Mama V was gone and would never return. She'd left me without any warning.

Rachael held me as my tears flowed. I tried hard to be strong, but I felt so weak as I packed up her belongings, looking for a place to begin and a place to start over again.

Rachel and her family carried everything in from the car, including what I had left of Mama V from our final days together. I couldn't look at it. I couldn't believe it was real. As I began to go through the house and package up all her belongings, I felt I was removing her from my life, like I was replacing her with something new. Although they were only things, they were all I had left of her—all I had to hold on to, all that reminded me of her love.

Once our loved ones are gone, we're left with the things that remind us of them. Memories that bring joy and tears despite the loneliness and pain. There's no right way or wrong way to grieve someone—there's just your way. Each person grieves differently. Some choose to hold on tighter, and others decide to let go. I struggled as I held tighter because I didn't want to let go of the things holding me captive to the pain I felt. I felt like letting go was giving up a part of me and letting go of Mama V. But I know Mama V will always be with me in my heart.

The truth is when people leave you, they never completely leave. Their bodies have been laid to rest, but their soul lives forever. Mama V battled an illness she could no longer fight as her body grew tired and weak. But her spirit lives on in the many memories held in my heart of her laughter and tears.

Mama V fought the good fight and has now won the reward for which God called her.

"I have fought the good fight, I have finished the race, I have kept the faith. Now there is in store for me the crown of righteousness, which the Lord, the righteous Judge, will award to me on that day—and not only to me but also to all who have longed for his appearing" (2 Timothy 4:7–8).

CHAPTER 13

MY SACRED JOURNEY

My faith continues to carry me through the storm as the world around me evolves at a rapid pace. People have become addicted to hurry. I told myself this didn't pertain to me because I live with a chronic illness that doesn't allow me to hurry.

But oh, how wrong I was! Although my body doesn't allow me to hurry physically, I'm constantly running emotionally, mentally, and spiritually. I often find myself running in a circle that leads me back to the pain and suffering I endure daily. I've learned that until I take the time to rest in Jesus, I can't hear His still, small voice speak to me. As a child, I often heard the saying that the more you hurry, the more you get behind. Today, I realize how true this statement is.

No matter how hard I try to run from my physical or mental pain, it's still there. Not until I rest in God's Word can I find peace and joy during my pain. The pain and suffering I endure would often overtake God's peace and joy in my life. I've learned not to rely on my strength but to lean into my weakness so Jesus can be strong in me. "My presence will go with you, and I will give you rest" (Exodus 33:14).

When an individual runs a marathon, they can stop along the way to get water to be refueled. As we run the marathon of life, we must stop and refuel ourselves with God's Word. Sitting in silence is a way of slowing ourselves and stopping our thoughts. It allows us to meditate on God and His plan for our lives. In Psalm 46, God tells us, "Be still, and know that I am God" (Psalm 46:10). He didn't tell us to hurry and get everything done but to be still. So, how does a world of hurry come to a roaring halt? We go to God!

Each of us has a place we go for rest—a place where we find God. I go to the beach or outdoors to be in nature. I'm a naturalist.

A naturalist loves God through the outdoors. I find peace, comfort, and strength in nature. I seek God by surrounding myself with all He has created as I gaze into the majestic sky and see the beauty of the clouds illuminated with a touch of light. They remind me of how Jesus's light shines into our darkness. As I hear the whisper of the breeze, my soul is soothed. As I hear the thunder, I hear the roar of a mighty king. As the sun caresses my skin, I feel God's love pour over me.

Psalm 23 reminds us that God is with us in nature and all that surrounds us. "The Lord is my shepherd; I shall not want. He makes me lie down in green pastures. He leads me beside still waters. He restores my soul. He leads me in paths of righteousness for his name's sake. Even though I walk through the valley of the shadow of death, I will fear no evil, for you are with me; your rod and your staff, they comfort me" (Psalm 23:1–4).

Nature is where I become one with God. Servant leadership is how I share God's love. A servant leader loves God by loving others. I'm drawn to love those who are hurting or in need.

Nature, people, and worship come together in unity, creating my sacred pathway and drawing me closer to God. Long walks on the beach with sand between my toes and waves crashing is what I envision heaven to be. A place that takes me away from all I endure here on earth and makes me focus on the serenity and peace God has given me.

I praise God continually through the songs of my heart and the dances of my feet as I incorporate all three pathways into my life. These pathways take me on a pilgrimage toward spiritual formation, where I draw closer to God and connect on a deeper level, becoming one with Him.

I've given my life to God as a willing vessel to be used for His calling on my life. Not until I began to follow the ways God had planned for my life was I able to see where He was leading me so I could lead others.

As I seek a deeper relationship with God, I'm in awe of how He connects with me throughout the day. Whether on the beach listening to the gentle waves crashing to the shore as the wind roars majestically, or loving on someone who is hurting, or at church worshipping God, He's there with me. The more I become like Christ, the closer I am to Christ.

Graduating from the seminary despite my medical challenges was another stepping stone along my life's journey. My health is a constant, uphill battle. In addition to the brain injury and chronic migraines, I've been diagnosed with an autoimmune disorder that attacks my organs and the tissue in my body. There's no cure; medical personnel continue to do all they can to help slow the process. School is a blessing and a struggle. I continually pray for God to show me the blessings in the battles as I do my best to keep my faith in the storm; each storm strengthens my faith and reminds me of my many blessings.

Shortly after graduating from seminary, I got accepted into IWU DeVoe Business School. I was excited about becoming Dr. Pebbles Wireman. Classes began with many challenges. The Doctor of Business Administration (DBA) program is a team-based program that works toward solving problems together. We were put together in a team of five students who worked hard together to prepare for our first residency in January 2022. We were excited about our team and project.

Each team presented their project before the students and faculty. We began as a strong team and went on to win the best presentation at the residency. The residency included moments of happiness, hard work, and fear as I embarked on this new chapter in my life. I loved my time with my chair and another student named Linsey. I knew they would both become a special part of my life. They both showed love and compassion as I battled through the weekend with my arm in a brace and fighting a migraine. Although I struggled through it, my health didn't divert me from doing my best and achieving all we had set out to do as a team.

But after we got home, something changed. Our team began to crumble. The words our team had agreed on—respect, integrity, clarity, and honesty (RICH)—were now the words that tore us apart. Our team was no longer the five people who set up our foundation of Team RICH. We grew apart with different goals along the way.

Many students didn't understand my disability, which created a cliff between us and we couldn't bridge our differences—The Disability Cliff. Students with disabilities are often left on the other side of the cliff, excluded from those around them.

People don't mean to exclude those who are disabled; they simply don't know how to include them.

As a student with a disability, I've felt the silent stares of those around me from projects that didn't include me. While many people hold standards of what they feel is normal, there are no ordinary people. We are in a world captured in the expectations of those around us and lost in the reality of who we are. "God created man in his own image, in the image of God he created him; male and female he created them." (Genesis 1:27). All of us are created in His image. Therefore, how can we be deceived by the expectations of those around us?

While people with disabilities endeavor to improve the quality of their lives, they are often limited by the people around them. The success of these people depends on the level of commitment from the community around them to create an inclusive environment. When people with disabilities are included, you'll find they value the same things as those who aren't disabled—God, family, friends, freedom, security, health, and peace.

I'm grateful for those who prayed for me across The Disability Cliff where I was abandoned. They helped me reach the other side and venture down the road less traveled. My friends Stacey and Cammie were my rocks during this time. They continued to encourage me through some major decisions as I was being led in another direction, which included leaving the DBA program.

Although I left the DBA program, I didn't leave my goals behind. Getting accepted into the Doctor of Education Program at IWU was the beginning of my newest journey.

When we are too busy, we are consumed by the world around us and are unable to see what's right in front of us. God showed me where I needed to be at that moment. He is opening new doors for The Mooky Project and ministering to children.

My health continued to decline while working on my EdD program to the point that I did not have the strength to go on.

Each day was a battle with my health. Tears flooded my eyes as I continued to push myself beyond what I was capable of.

Then my dad's health began to worsen rapidly. Friends became my anchors, providing meals, calls, cards, and many visits in front of the fire at Dina's house, the place I ran to when I wanted to hide from the pain and escape the world I lived in. She gave me space with the assurance of comfort and support, reminding me that I was not alone. That God was there. I left her house one rainy night with tears flooding my face as the song "Jesus Lover of My Soul" reminded me He will never let me go. With no strength left to give, I called out to Him. I could hear Him whisper to me in the silence of the day "Come to me, all who labor and are heavy laden, and I will give you rest" (Matthew 11:28).

I didn't have time to rest. My classes consumed my mind and body. I had to step back and come to a complete stop!

That is when I heard the still, soft voice of the Holy Spirit speak to me. *You have been on this journey for a long time and while the end is near, there is a detour to the place you need to be for this moment in time.*

CHAPTER 14

FINDING FAITH IN THE STORM

On a cold, stormy night last spring, I walked down the long hallway to my dad's hospital room and found him lying silently. I climbed onto the mattress beside him and played gentle music in the background like any other night. But this wasn't like any other night. My dad slowly drifted away as his vitals began to fade. I clasped his hand as the moments passed. My heart was left so empty and feeling so alone as I wrote this final letter to my dad before I drove away.

> Dad,
> I will never forget day I got the text from Ron that you had fallen and were rushed to the hospital. I prepared myself for anything. Or I thought I had until I saw you lying there in so much pain. There was nothing I could do but hold your hand. I wanted to take the pain from you. I wanted to hold you and tell you everything would be all right. But deep down in my heart, I knew this was part of your journey.
> The next morning, we all surrounded you with love as we waited for them to take you back to surgery. We fought back the tears, realizing each moment could be our last with you. I could hear the clock ticking as I felt my heart pounding

through my chest. I saw a tear slide down your face as I kissed your forehead before they wheeled you away.

The hours passed by slowly as we waited. Memories flowed through our minds with love and laughter. The past few months I had with you are the times I will cherish forever. Although your mind had begun to slip away, you continued to love us in every way. I can still hear you chuckle as we talked about memories of the past and embraced the memories of the moment.

You touched so many lives in these past few months. Each of the nurses bonded with you and shared special moments as we sat with you. They brought laughter amid our tears.

We didn't know if we'd see you after surgery. We didn't know what to expect. The doctor prepared us for the worst, or so I thought. But I wasn't prepared to watch you suffer as you did in these final days.

A bit of hope came with every syringe of broth you drank, but mine was a selfish hope. I wasn't ready to let you go. I wasn't ready to say goodbye. I wanted everything to go back to the way it was before the fall. I wanted everything to go back to the way it was before you got sick. I wanted to have my dad back.

The days became longer, and the nights became darker as the days passed. Oh, what I would give to hear you say my name once again—to hear your voice and see you smile. The darkness overtook me as I watched you lie there and suffer. The silence overtook the air and left me paralyzed to the pain as I left your room for the last time.

I love you, Dad! You will always remain in my heart. This is not goodbye. It is "until we meet again." You will always live on in my heart.

Your Baby Girl

FINDING FAITH IN THE STORM

Sometimes, I still feel like I'm in a dream I can't escape. My heart doesn't know how to express it all. I am lost to the pain and grief I felt that day. Wishing I had more time to say all the things I never said. Writing letters to my dad has become my therapy and escape. Although my dad will never read these letters, they somehow bring hope and healing and allow me to keep the love for my dad alive in my heart as I fight the memories of that stormy night when I walked down the long hallway to my dad's room for the last time.

My heart kept growing heavier as time passed. The darkness began to overpower me. The world continued around me while I became paralyzed by the pain that has brought my world to a complete stop.

No one sees my silent tears or hears my heart cry as I sit and hold his hand in mine. Dad, you taught us to be strong in the face of adversity and never to give up. Your love will carry us through until we meet again.

As the raindrops fall outside, my tears continue to flow and create a puddle. I am isolated in a dark room filled with family. My heart is overtaken with pain and sorrow as I cradle myself in the palm of Jesus's hands.

As my dad wrapped his hand around mine, I envisioned myself wrapped in the palm of Jesus's hand. He gently wrapped his four fingers around me, protecting me from the storm. A light peeked through my darkness, illuminating the love that was around me. The love that surrounded my dad as his children loved him through his transition from this life to the next.

The thunder rolled and the lightning flashed as we watched my dad struggle to take his last breath, I saw the packaging die (his body) as the gift inside (his soul) rose to be with his Father in heaven. We are all gifts, waiting to be unwrapped and taken to the Father who gave us the gift of eternal life.

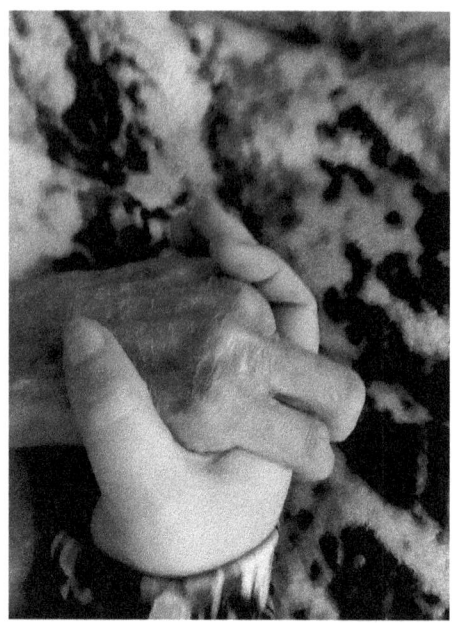

God has used these past weeks during the editing process of this book to bring healing as I relived those last moments with my dad. I can now look back with love instead of such unbearable pain of the memories of him suffering so deeply. My grief has changed and now comes from a place of love for him instead of sorrow for all he had endured. I don't need to grieve for him anymore. I still grieve for my own loss. But I can now cherish the special moments in that grief—the laughter and the tears.

Jesus continued to hold me in the palm of His hand, reminding me He is there and will never leave me. His presence consumed me from the inside out, taking my every breath and filling me anew again. Jesus poured His love over me like an ocean of water flooding my soul. He took me back to that day long ago when He first came into my life. He reminded me that I'm never alone, and He will always be with me to carry me through another storm.

My life has been filled with many valleys and hilltops. Yet I have peace in knowing that through every storm, God has promised to be with me.

FINDING FAITH IN THE STORM

In those times when I'm strong, He walks beside me, directing and guiding me. In those times when I'm weak, He carries me in His loving arms. He never promised us we wouldn't suffer, but He did promise He would never leave us. I love the English Standard Version of Joel 3:10. "Let the weak say 'I am a warrior.'"

I am a warrior for Christ no matter what I face.

Continuing to keep the faith in the storms ...

PEBBLES' SENIOR PICTURE

**PEBBLES AND DEBRA REUNITED
TWENTY YEARS LATER**

PEBBLES, BROTHER RON, AND DONNA

PEBBLES AT IWU GRADUATION 2018

MOOKY AT IWU GRADUATION 2018

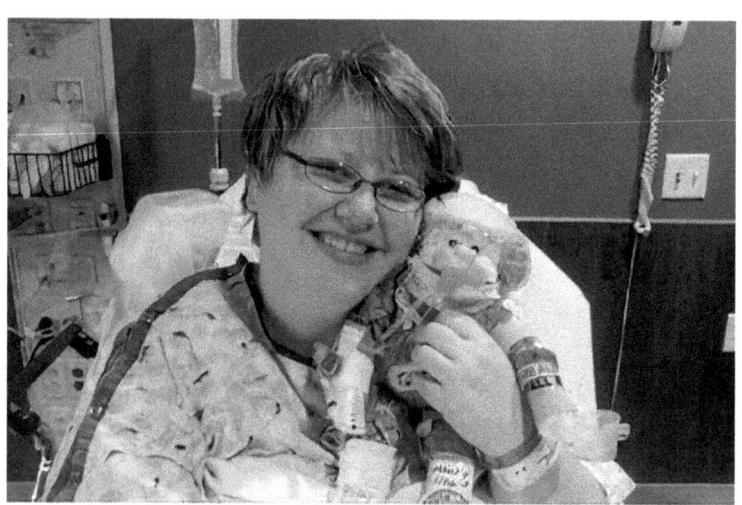

PEBBLES WITH MOOKY 2018

PEBBLES AND MAMA V

MOOKY AND PRINCESS BELLE

PEBBLES AND PRINCESS BELLE

DONNA, PEBBLES, PRINCESS BELLE AND MAMA V

ABOUT THE AUTHOR

In the summer before her last year of high school, Pebbles Wireman sustained multiple injuries in a motor vehicle accident, including a traumatic brain injury. Three years later, a second accident exacerbated her previous injuries, leaving her with debilitating, life-changing diagnoses. Despite the physical and mental challenges, many surgeries, and hospitalizations, Pebbles completed a bachelor's degree in communications and a master's degree in ministry. She now shares her story of grit, determination, and faith through her speaking and writing. Although Pebbles battles multiple illnesses, she has not permitted them to stop her from fulfilling her lifelong dream of becoming an author and ministering to children in the hospital.